The
SUPER SMART
HUMAN
BODY
Activity Book

By Lisa Regan

Illustrated by
Isabel Muñoz

ARCTURUS

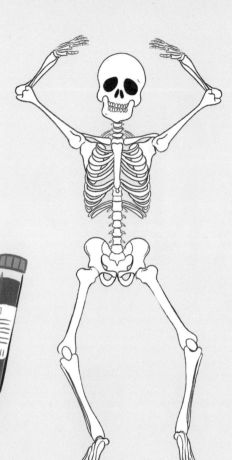

ARCTURUS

This edition published in 2022 by Arcturus Publishing Limited
26/27 Bickels Yard, 151–153 Bermondsey Street,
London SE1 3HA

Author: Lisa Regan
Illustrator: Isabel Muñoz
Editor: Violet Peto
Consultant: Dr. Kristina Routh
Designer: Sarah Fountain
Managing Editor: Joe Harris
Design Manager: Jessica Holliland

ISBN: 978-1-3988-1533-9
CH010095NT
Supplier 29, Date 0322, PI 00000705

Printed in China

What is STEM?

STEM is a world-wide initiative
that aims to cultivate an
interest in Science, Technology,
Engineering, and Mathematics,
in an effort to promote these
disciplines to as wide a variety of
students as possible.

YOUR AMAZING BODY

From brains and bones to senses and cells, this activity book takes you on a fact-packed tour of your body. There are over 50 fun puzzles to solve and many mind-boggling facts to discover along the way!

Have you ever wondered what causes hiccups, why we dream, or how fast a sneeze can travel?

Turn the page to find out everything you ever wanted to know and more about your amazing body!

Did you know?
Your brain shrinks as you get older!

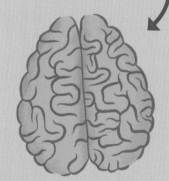

Did you know?
Your body contains 206 bones!

HAIR AND THERE

What better way to begin our exploration of the human body, than with a festival of fabulous facial hair? Match these terrific 'taches into pairs and find the one that's truly unique.

Facial hair sprouts when testosterone levels increase. The amount of facial hair a person grows is influenced by their genes.

Beards tend to be bushier in the summer because of seasonal changes in hormone levels.

Some people are afraid of beards! Their condition even has a name—pogonophobia. Conversely, pogonophilia is a love of beards.

Facial hair fashions change in the western world. At some points in history, facial hair has been seen as a sign of power. At others, a clean-shaven look was preferred. In Victorian Britain, men were so keen to have whiskers that they would buy false beards if they couldn't grow one naturally.

SKELETON SEARCH

There are 206 bones in a full-grown human body. Can you match the bones shown in the key to the bones in the skeleton?

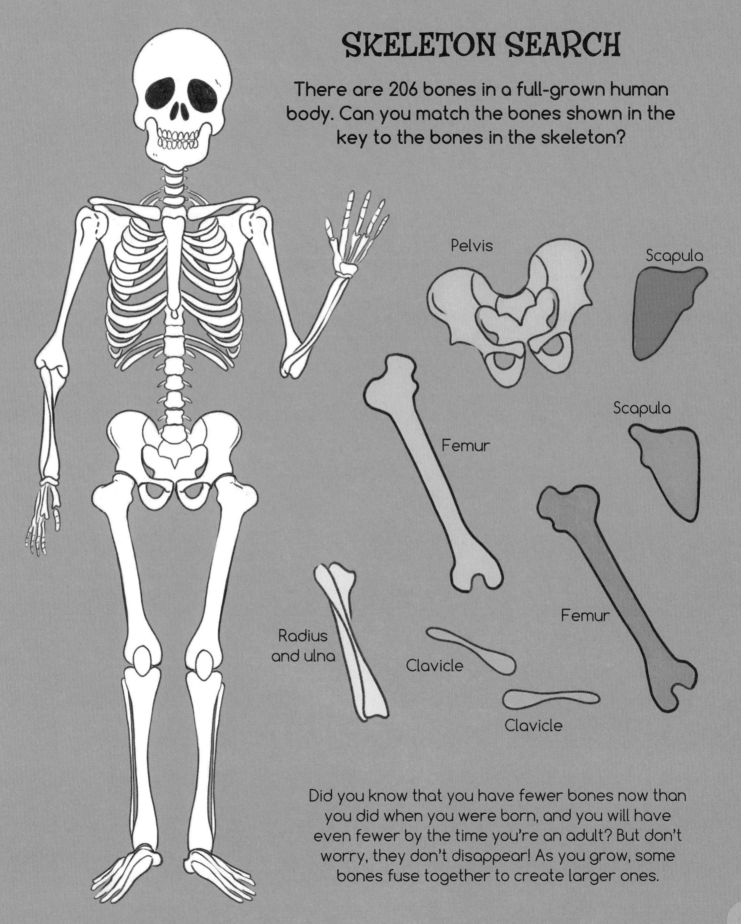

Pelvis

Scapula

Scapula

Femur

Femur

Radius and ulna

Clavicle

Clavicle

Did you know that you have fewer bones now than you did when you were born, and you will have even fewer by the time you're an adult? But don't worry, they don't disappear! As you grow, some bones fuse together to create larger ones.

TEMPERATURE CHECK

Your parents or a doctor may take your temperature to see if you're sick. How many thermometers can you count in this jumbled pile?

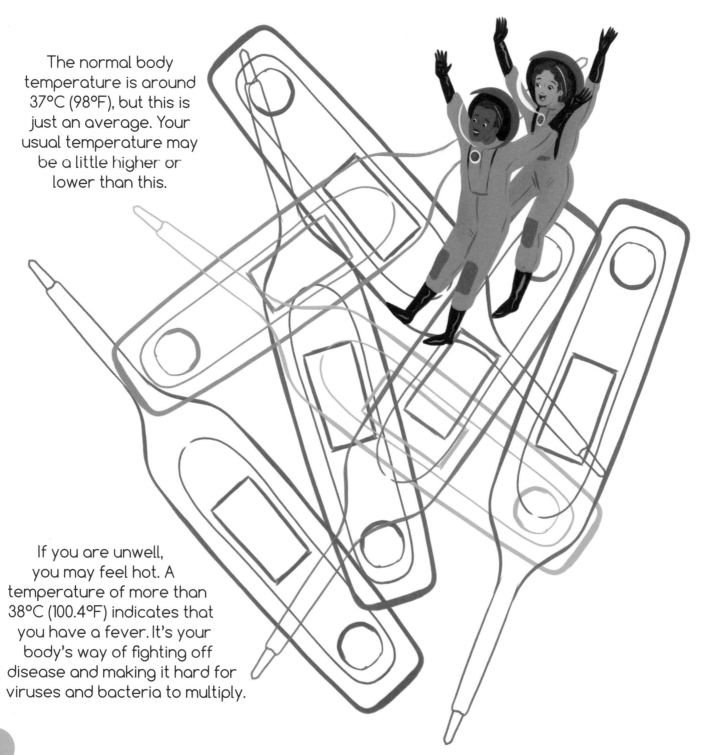

The normal body temperature is around 37°C (98°F), but this is just an average. Your usual temperature may be a little higher or lower than this.

If you are unwell, you may feel hot. A temperature of more than 38°C (100.4°F) indicates that you have a fever. It's your body's way of fighting off disease and making it hard for viruses and bacteria to multiply.

THE GOOD GUYS

Your body contains many different types of bacteria. Not all of them are bad. Some, such as those in your digestive system, have an important job to do. See if you can find the good guys among all the ones below. How many are there of each?

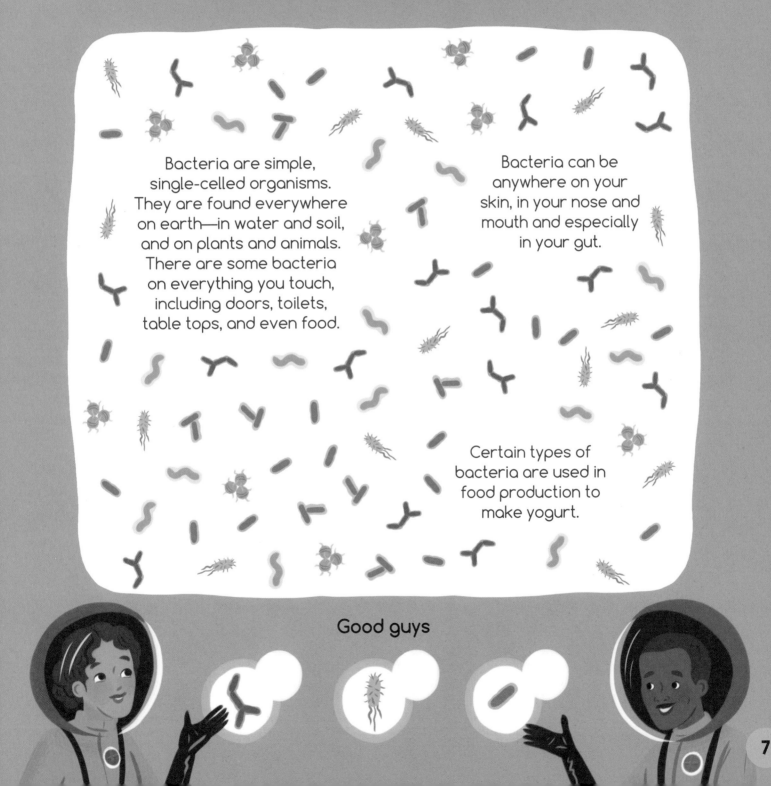

Bacteria are simple, single-celled organisms. They are found everywhere on earth—in water and soil, and on plants and animals. There are some bacteria on everything you touch, including doors, toilets, table tops, and even food.

Bacteria can be anywhere on your skin, in your nose and mouth and especially in your gut.

Certain types of bacteria are used in food production to make yogurt.

Good guys

DREAM TIME

Scientists are still unsure why we dream. One reason could be that it helps the brain process emotions and experiences. Look carefully at the two pictures and find ten differences between them.

Scientists think that dreams could happen because of chemical changes that take place in the brain when we sleep.

FEELING NERVE-Y

The human body contains billions of odd-looking nerve cells. Each has a main body with lots of arms branching off it. Can you find one nerve cell here that isn't quite the same as all the others?

Nerve cells are also called neurons. They are connected to each other by thin threads and carry electrical signals.

Some nerve cells carry messages around your body, and can be over 1 m (3 ft) long.

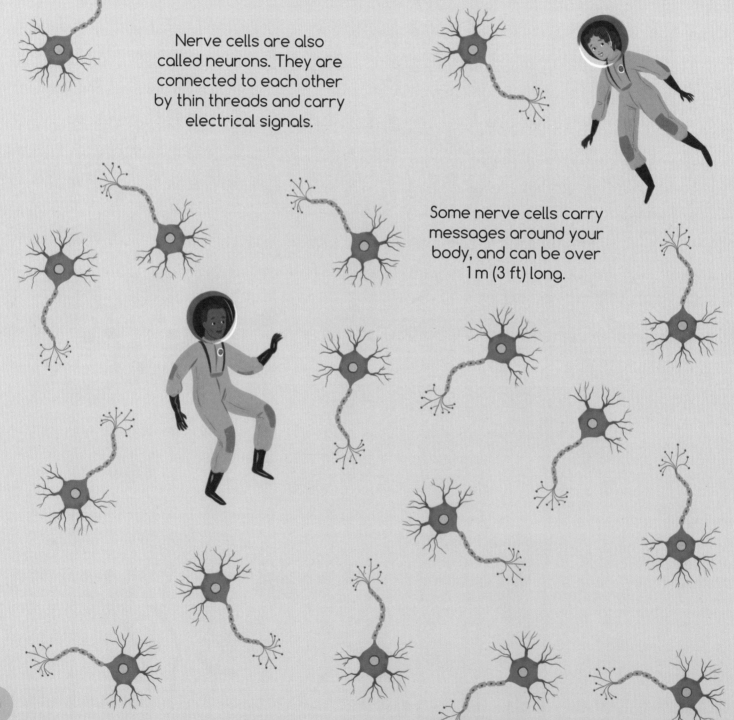

GETTING OLD

Getting older has an effect on the human body. Older people are more likely to have health and mobility problems, and struggle with their hearing and eyesight. Can you work out who is the oldest of all the people here?

* Jim is older than Betty and Ernest.
* Anjali and Janet are younger than Ernest.
* Ernest is younger than Betty and older than Claude.
* The second-oldest person is female.
* Janet is older than Anjali but younger than Claude.

The study of getting older is called gerontology.

FOOD FOR THOUGHT

We get the energy we need from our food and drink. About half of that energy is used for growing, healing, and keeping our body at the right temperature. The rest is needed for physical activities, from dancing and running to cleaning and playing.

Bananas contain lots of carbs (to give you energy) and potassium which is good for your heart. How many bananas can you count?

Bright red fruit and vegetables can help to protect your body from disease. How many different ones can you name here?

Onions, garlic, and leeks all belong to the same plant family. Research shows they're good for your skin and hair, and to help prevent some diseases. Look for all three in the picture.

Cheese and other dairy foods provide calcium and protein for strong bones and teeth. Can you spot four types of cheese?

INS-EYE-DER VIEW

Tears help to clean your eyes and keep them moist, even if you aren't crying. A few tears flow every time you blink. Can you guide this teardrop across this eye to give it a good clean?

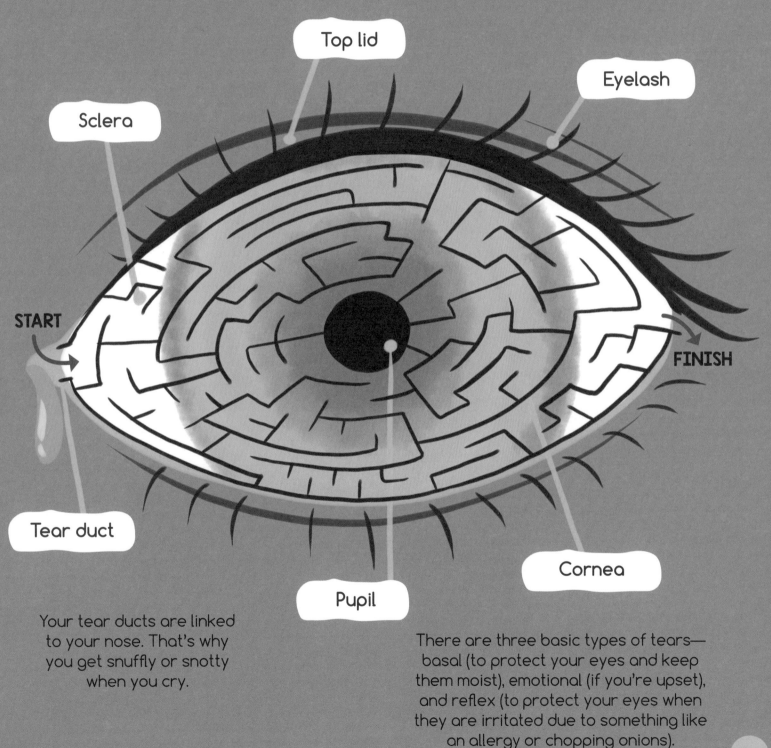

Your tear ducts are linked to your nose. That's why you get snuffly or snotty when you cry.

There are three basic types of tears—basal (to protect your eyes and keep them moist), emotional (if you're upset), and reflex (to protect your eyes when they are irritated due to something like an allergy or chopping onions).

SUPER SNEEZE

An average sneeze reaches speeds of up to 160km/hr (100 mph). Yuck! Study this sneeze and find three germs that don't match any of the others.
Which germ is the most common?

Scientists have discovered that a sneeze can travel about 8 m (27 ft). That's nearly as far as the long jump world record.

GOOD BLOOD

Blood travels around your body in blood vessels. They carry blood from the heart to the rest of the body, and then back again, in a continuous cycle. Blood contains different things that perform different jobs. Get your pens and pencils and bring this cross-section of the blood stream to life, using the key.

Plasma makes up over half of your blood. It is clear but yellow-ish and carries the platelets and red and white blood cells.

Red blood cells carry oxygen. Their shape is designed to hold as much oxygen as possible.

White blood cells are part of your immune system to help fight disease and infection.

Vein valves prevent the blood from flowing in the wrong direction.

Platelets join together to form a blood clot. They stop you from bleeding if you cut or graze your skin. They are the smallest type of blood cell.

Key

red blood cell

white blood cell

platelet

REVEALING REMAINS

Archaeologists study human remains to learn about people through history. The human skeleton reveals all kinds of clues, even hundreds of years after death. Which of the boxes contains all of the parts uncovered in the dig?

The skull and pelvis usually reveal whether the person is male or female.

A
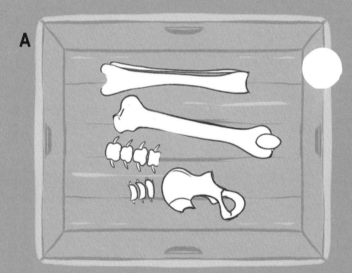

B
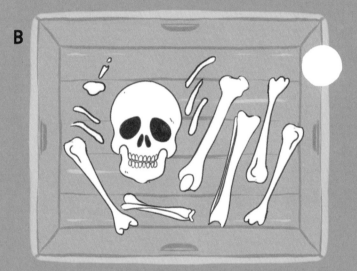

C
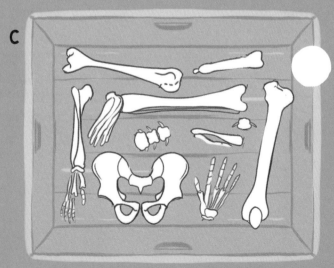

D
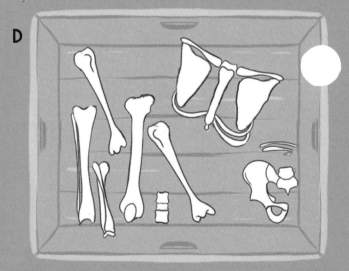

FACE FACTS!

Do you know the name for the bit that separates your nostrils from each other? Or the name for the groove above your top lip? Find out below!

ASAKKEPYFYFTOOUDMD

PHGEIGELCTRNUSMNCS

Cross out any letter that appears more than once in each thought bubble. Use the remaining letters to spell the body bits!

Muscles attached to the skin on your face allow you to show how you're feeling with expressions such as a frown, raised eyebrows, or a smile.

Dimples are genetic and are caused by a shortened muscle.

FAMILY PORTRAIT

A family will be made up of several generations. Which of the tiles below are not from the family portrait on the next page?

A generation is defined by the number of years it takes to be born and reach adulthood. A family generation is typically around 20-30 years. Your parents are a different generation from you, and your grandparents are the generation before your parents.

Improvements in living conditions and healthcare have allowed people to live for longer. By 2050, the number of people over 60 will be more than double what it was in 2015.

On average, women live between six and eight years longer than men.

Last century, people's life expectancy (the average life span) increased dramatically. In developed countries it rose from around 50 to over 75 years. As people live longer, more and more children will know their grandparents and even their great-grandparents.

GOING TO EXTREMES

Your hands and feet are amazing. They are remarkably similar in their bone structure, even though they perform different tasks. Work out what each one, plus a bulging biceps, is worth so you can answer the final question below.

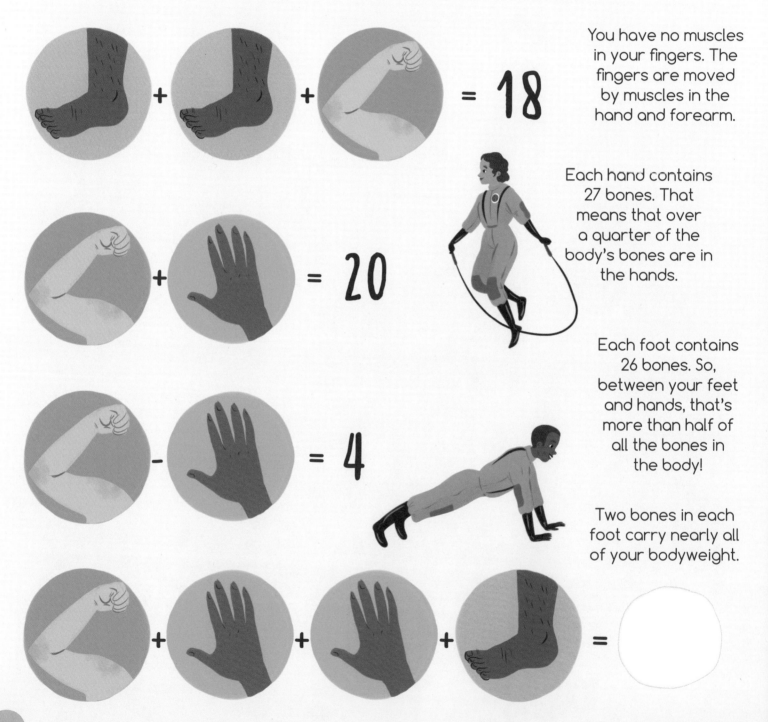

You have no muscles in your fingers. The fingers are moved by muscles in the hand and forearm.

Each hand contains 27 bones. That means that over a quarter of the body's bones are in the hands.

Each foot contains 26 bones. So, between your feet and hands, that's more than half of all the bones in the body!

Two bones in each foot carry nearly all of your bodyweight.

INSIDE A CELL

The body can be broken down into organs, which are made of tissue, which is a group of cells. Study the two pictures of a cell and see if you can spot six differences.

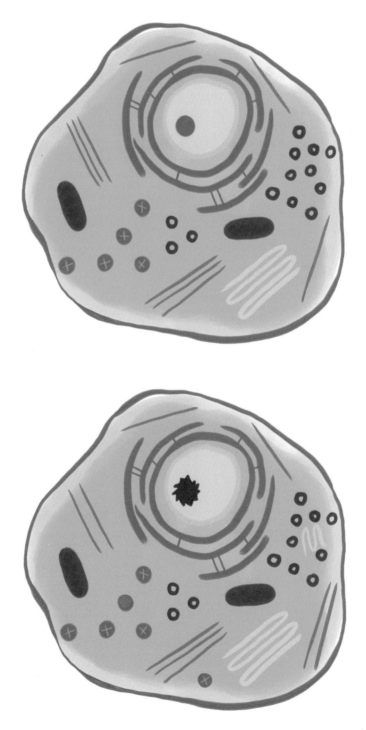

Human cells contain structures called **organelles**. These organelles have different and special jobs within the cell.

BRAIN FREEZE!

Ouch! That first taste of ice cream can bring on a headache. Don't worry, it happens to a lot of people. Use the logic clues to find out which ice cream Maria is eating.

* She has ordered more than one scoop.
* It isn't in a glass.
* She didn't choose strawberry ice cream.

Brain-freeze happens when nerves behind your nose and mouth sense something cold. They send a message to your brain which makes some blood vessels narrow, causing a headache.

WHO NOSE?

You have about 10 million smell receptors inside your nose, allowing you to recognize thousands and thousands of smells. Follow the lines to work out what Megan has caught a whiff of!

Scent molecules travel through the air and into your nose, where they trigger the receptors which then pass messages to your brain. Scientists think our brains can identify anything from 10,000 to 1 trillion different smells!

Smell, like your other senses, is there to help you stay safe. It acts as a warning if something is likely to harm you, like smoke from a burning house, or food that has gone bad.

SLEEPWALKING

Some people are able to get up and walk around even when they are asleep. Known as sleepwalking, it is more common in children than in adults. Help to guide this sleepwalker safely back to bed without bumping into anything!

We cycle through different types of sleep during the night. To begin with, we sleep lightly. As our muscles relax more, we sink into a deeper sleep. REM sleep is the stage where most dreaming happens.

Sleepwalking usually takes place during deep sleep. It is most likely to happen in the first few hours after falling asleep.

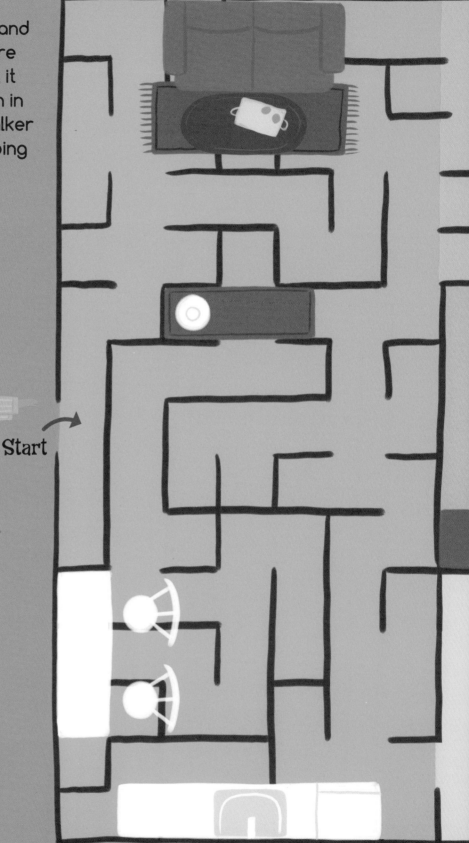

Start

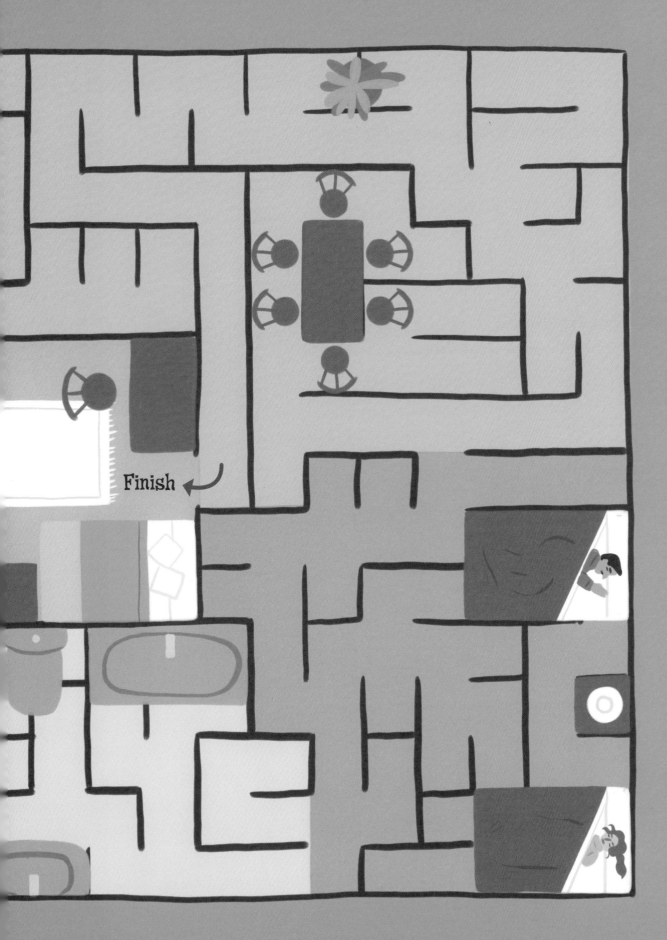

Finish

A BALANCED DIET

It is important that we eat healthily, with a wide range of different foods so that we get all the nutrients our body needs. Work out what each fruit is worth on these scales, using the lemon as a starting point.

A balanced diet includes proteins, fats, and carbohydrates. Protein helps us grow and repair ourselves. Fats store energy. Carbohydrates also give us energy. Fruits and vegetables help us digest our food so we can get rid of waste properly, and they contain the vitamins and minerals that we need.

= 5   =   =   =

LOVELY LOBES

The brain has different areas for doing different jobs. These areas are known as lobes. Use the key to shade in and label each lobe.

Key:

A = frontal lobe
B = parietal lobe
C = temporal lobe
D = occipital lobe
E = cerebellum

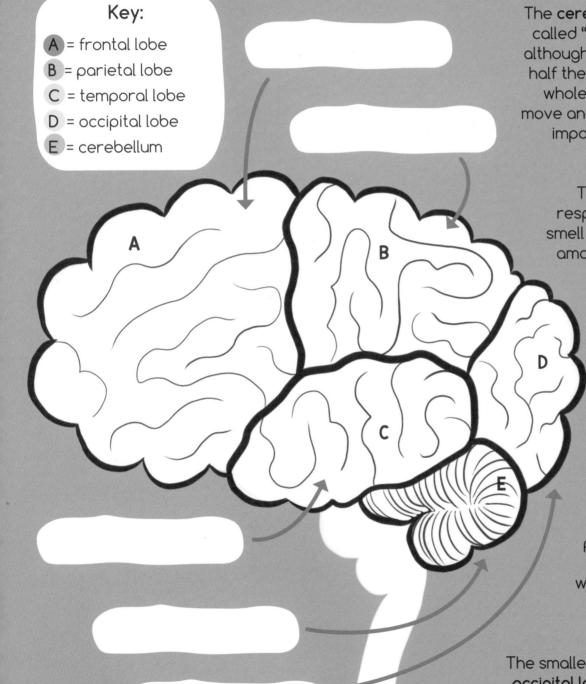

The **cerebellum** is sometimes called "the little brain" and, although small, contains over half the total neurons in the whole brain. It helps you move and balance, and is also important for speech.

The **frontal lobe** is responsible for speech, smell and problem-solving, among many other things.

The **temporal lobe** is the part of the brain that is closest to our ears. It processes sound received by our ears and allows us to understand language and verbal information.

The **parietal lobe** processes sensory information to do with touch, taste, and temperature.

The smallest lobe is the **occipital lobe**. Its main function is interpreting information from the eyes and turning it into vision.

FIND THE FINGERS

Humans have small ridges on the skin of their fingers. They help create friction so things don't slip out of your grasp. They form patterns that are totally unique for every person, so can be used to identify people—for phone ID, or at a crime scene.

Find a match for each of the five fingerprints on the hand. Which two prints were not made by this person?

Identical twins don't have identical fingerprints. Fingerprints are formed before a baby is born.

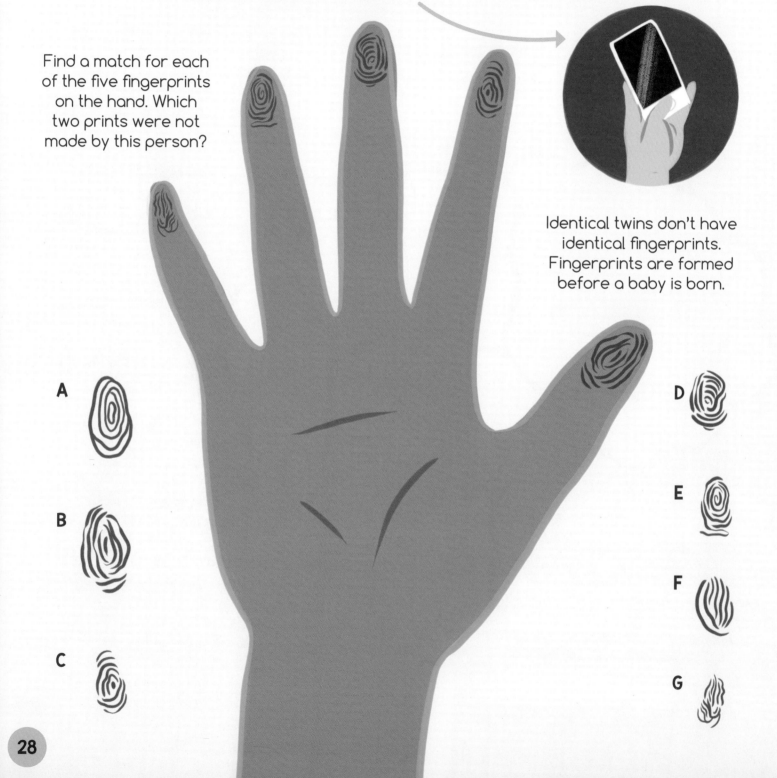

A

B

C

D

E

F

G

CELL COUNT

The brain contains different types of cells. The most common are neurons. Use your brain power to work out the answers below.

* Half of the cells are firing at once. Draw a star on 50 percent of them.
* Now mark a cross on one fifth of the unmarked cells.
* Put a circle on a quarter of the remaining blank cells.
* How many cells have no markings on them?

The average adult human brain was said to contain around 100 billion neurons. However, scientists continue to study the brain to see if this is accurate, and think it may actually contain billions less than that.

MIRROR IMAGE

Sadie has started to lose her baby teeth. Which of the smaller images is what she sees when she looks in the mirror?

Babies have teeth even before they are born, but they don't usually begin to show until they are 6 months old.

Most children have their first set of teeth, called milk teeth, by the time they're 3. These begin to fall out to make way for their adult teeth.

A

B

C

USE YOUR HEAD

Many of your sense receptors are found on your head. Can you work out how much each one is worth and do the equation using the calculations below?

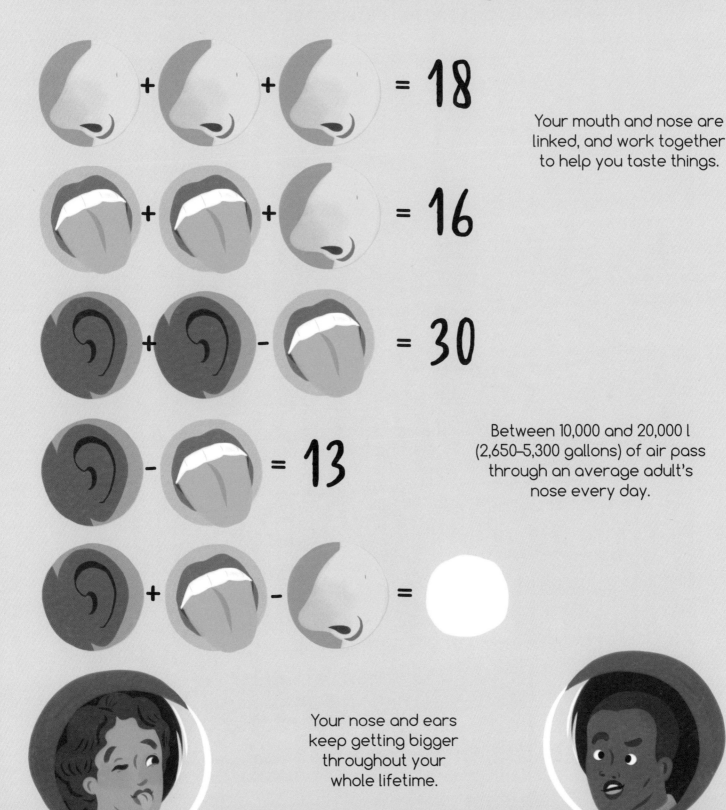

Your mouth and nose are linked, and work together to help you taste things.

Between 10,000 and 20,000 l (2,650–5,300 gallons) of air pass through an average adult's nose every day.

Your nose and ears keep getting bigger throughout your whole lifetime.

ADRENALINE RUSH

That fizzy feeling you get when you're scared or excited? It's caused by a hormone called adrenaline. Look carefully at the two pictures and find ten differences between them.

The **adrenal glands** release adrenaline into the bloodstream. It travels to your vital organs increasing your heart rate and boosting the oxygen supply to your brain and muscles.

GET MOVING!

There are all kinds of fun ways to exercise and strengthen your body. Which activities get you moving? Find out what these people have been doing, and where they do it, by using the clues.

* One of the girls plays hockey.
* The hockey team plays in the gym.
* Ethan does his sport at school.
* The swimmer doesn't swim outdoors.
* Teresa doesn't visit the gym.

	Hockey	Basketball	Swimming
Ethan			
Angela			
Teresa			

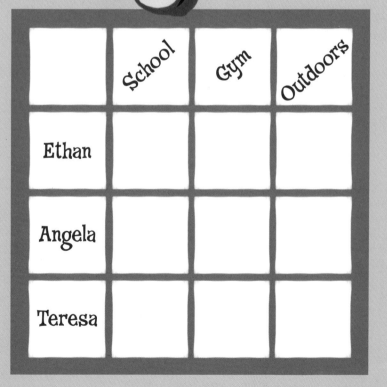

	School	Gym	Outdoors
Ethan			
Angela			
Teresa			

Physical activity such as swimming, running, hockey, and basketball are all aerobic exercises. They all encourage your body to use oxygen to help your large muscles burn fuel and move.

34

GOOD HABITS

Experts suggest you should brush twice a day to protect your teeth from plaque and decay. Find a path through this grid, following the brushes in this order each time:

blue   red   yellow

You can move left and right and up and down, but not diagonally.

Start

Finish

There are 32 teeth in a full set of adult teeth. Once they are damaged or lost, they can't grow back. That is why it is so important to look after them.

Brushing your teeth helps remove food and plaque (a sticky white coating that contains bacteria). These bacteria produce acids that can break down tooth enamel and cause tooth decay.

SEEING DOUBLE

Scientists carry out experiments to see if they can clone cells. Cloning means making an exact genetic copy of a living thing. In 1996, scientists successfully cloned a sheep. Can you spot which two of these sheep are identical?

A

B

C

D

Cloning may be useful for treating human diseases. It is also hoped that cloning will allow scientists to grow healthy tissue, in the laboratory, to replace damaged or dead tissue.

E

F

G

H

I

EYE-DENTIFICATION

The ring around your pupil is called the iris, and is determined by your genes. No two people (not even twins) have the same iris pattern. Study these eyes carefully and then turn the page. Which ones do you remember?

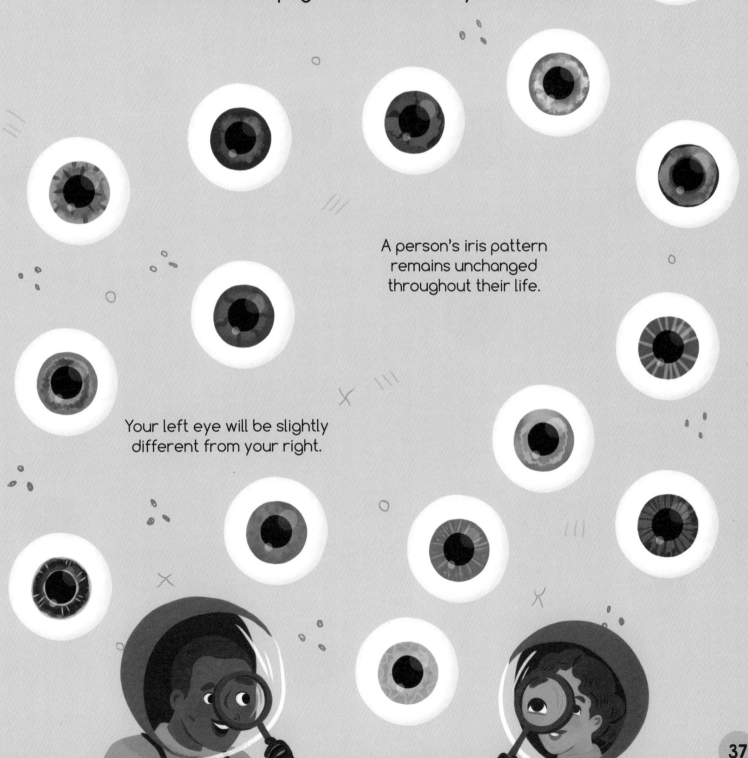

A person's iris pattern remains unchanged throughout their life.

Your left eye will be slightly different from your right.

PART 2 OF EYE-DENTIFICATION

Because all iris patterns are unique, they can be used for visual identification. Iris recognition technology can be used instead of a password for computers and smart phones, and as security at border control or in business.

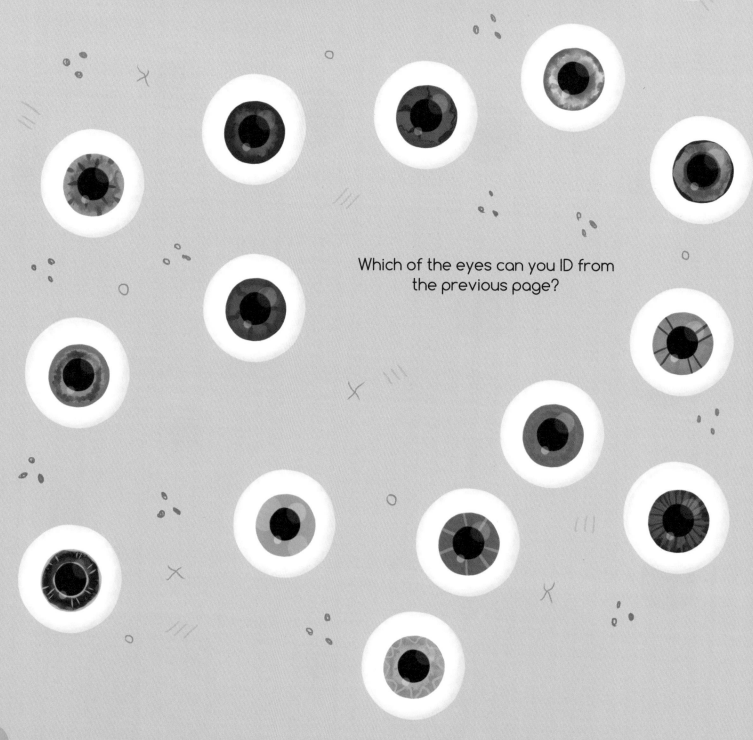

Which of the eyes can you ID from the previous page?

BAG O' BONES

The skeletal system acts as a frame for your whole body. It is made up of hard bone and firm springy cartilage. Which is the only group of letters that can be rearranged to spell SKELETON?

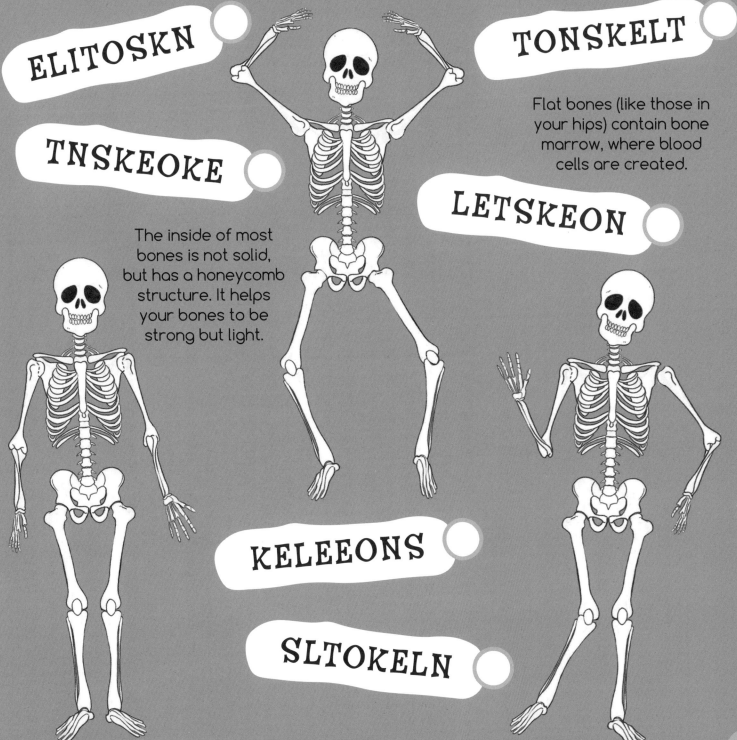

ELITOSKN

TONSKELT

Flat bones (like those in your hips) contain bone marrow, where blood cells are created.

TNSKEOKE

LETSKEON

The inside of most bones is not solid, but has a honeycomb structure. It helps your bones to be strong but light.

KELEEONS

SLTOKELN

OUT OF CONTROL

Diseases can be caused by bacteria reproducing and spreading in the body. Medicines called antibiotics can fight them by stopping the bacteria from growing. See if you can spot the odd one out in each group of bacteria.

Examples of bacterial diseases include pneumonia, meningitis, salmonella (a type of food poisoning), and cholera. Not all diseases are caused by bacteria.

SHIVERS DOWN YOUR SPINE

The spine isn't one bone; it is made of a total of 26 bones. Together, they form a column from the base of your skull to your pelvis. Can you find which bones are missing from the collection on this page?

The spine needs:

* 7 neck bones
  (called **cervical vertebrae**)

* 12 chest bones
  (called **thoracic vertebrae**)

* 5 lower back bones
  (called **lumbar vertebrae**)

* 1 sacrum

* 1 coccyx

UH-OH!

This X-ray shows a lot of items that really shouldn't be found on the inside! Which of the tiles on the next page are not from the picture below?

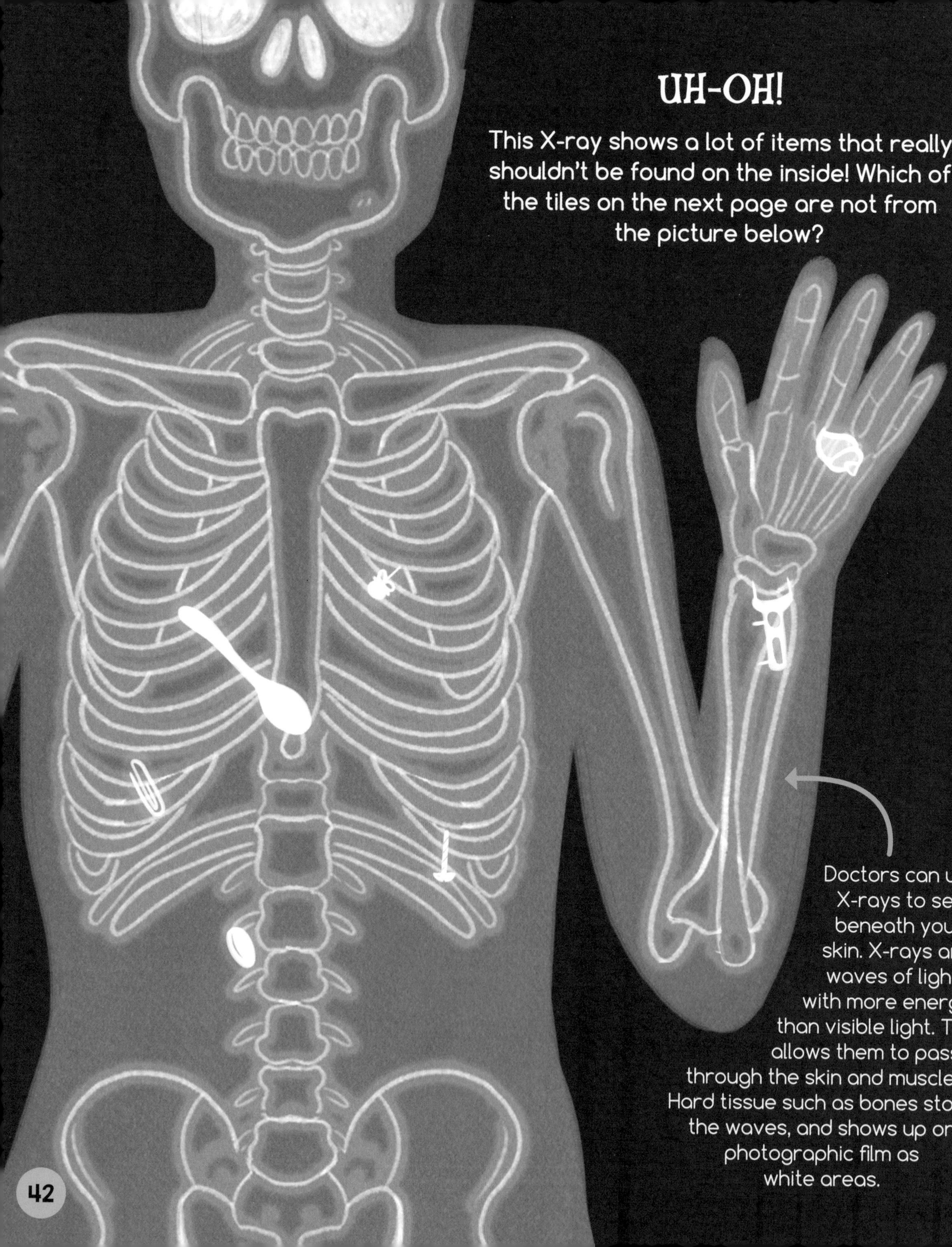

Doctors can use X-rays to see beneath your skin. X-rays are waves of light with more energy than visible light. This allows them to pass through the skin and muscle. Hard tissue such as bones stops the waves, and shows up on photographic film as white areas.

A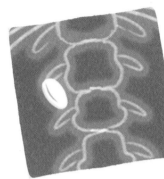

B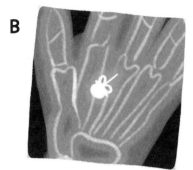

C

D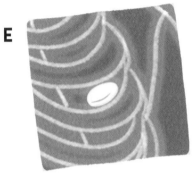

E

X-rays were discovered in 1895 by German scientist William Röntgen. They are mostly carried out in hospital X-ray departments by specialists called radiographers. You may also have your mouth X-rayed at the dentist so they can study your teeth.

Bones aren't the only thing that can be seen on X-rays. Other hard items such as metal also show up. Doctors can use this to find things that people have accidentally swallowed or lodged under their skin. X-ray images also show metal pins and screws that have been used to fix broken bones.

F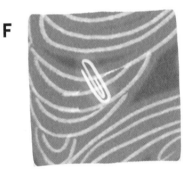

G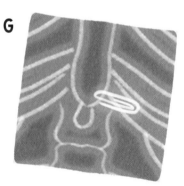

H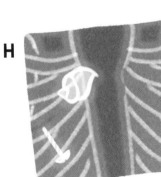

I

J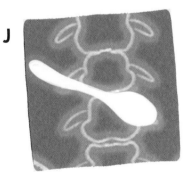

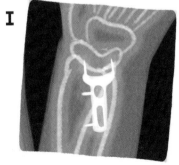

TWISTED!

This spiral ladder shows the molecular structure of DNA.
Study the main one and then find which of the smaller
ones is the same DNA strand, but upside down.

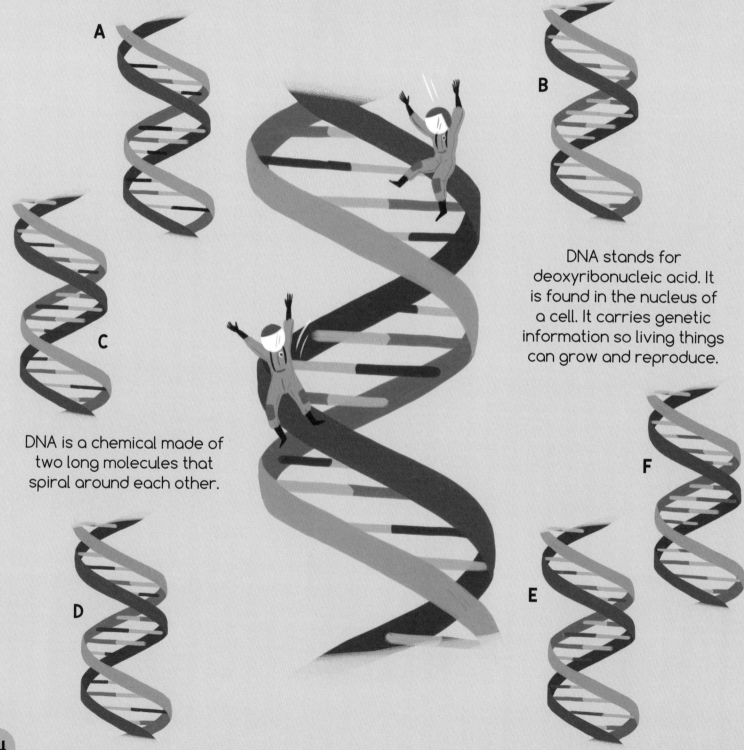

DNA stands for
deoxyribonucleic acid. It
is found in the nucleus of
a cell. It carries genetic
information so living things
can grow and reproduce.

DNA is a chemical made of
two long molecules that
spiral around each other.

THE BEST MEDICINE

Medicines can fight diseases and help people to feel better when they are ill. Can you find the bottles that have been prescribed here?

* A clear bottle with a red label and blue lid.
* A brown bottle with a yellow label and a brown lid.
* A blue bottle with a white label and white lid.

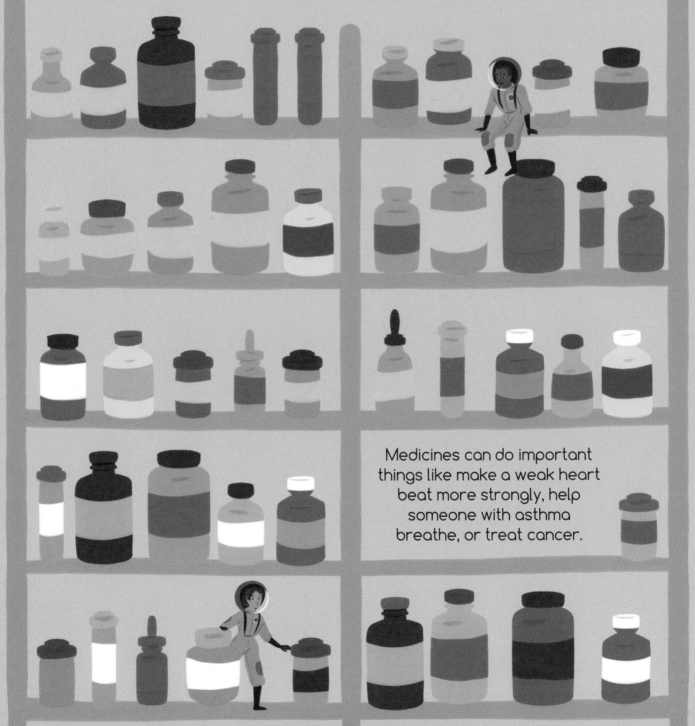

Medicines can do important things like make a weak heart beat more strongly, help someone with asthma breathe, or treat cancer.

ALL CUT UP

Your teeth are different shapes, like kitchen knives, to perform different tasks—for cutting, tearing, ripping, grinding, and slicing. Count the different types of teeth in this jumbled pile.

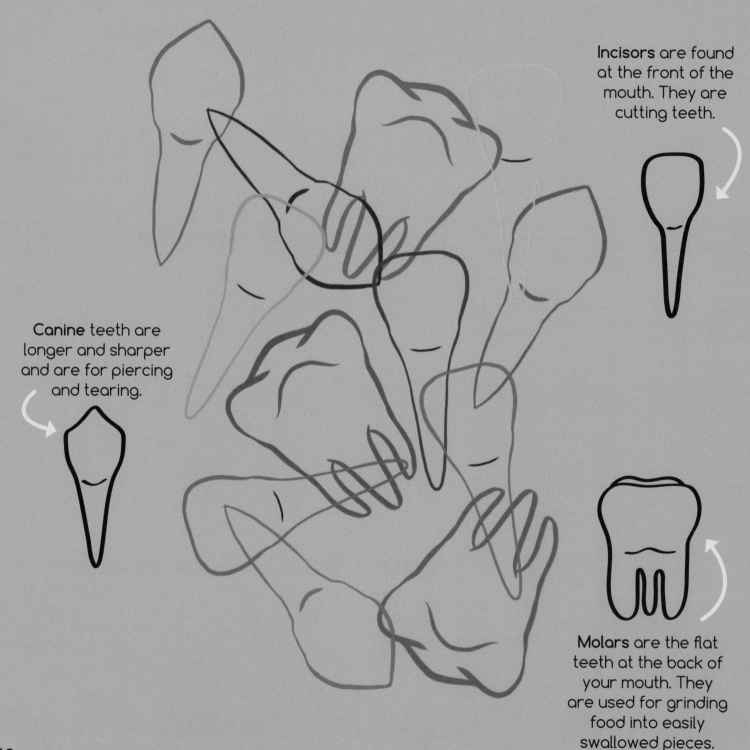

Incisors are found at the front of the mouth. They are cutting teeth.

Canine teeth are longer and sharper and are for piercing and tearing.

Molars are the flat teeth at the back of your mouth. They are used for grinding food into easily swallowed pieces.

GETTING A REACTION

Allergies are your body's reaction to something that disagrees with it.
You might get a rash, red eyes, sneezes, swelling, or a shortness of breath.
Use the clues to work out what allergy each of these people have.

An **allergy** is your body's immune system over-reacting to something that's usually harmless. Your body responds by trying to fight it, triggering annoying or even dangerous symptoms.

* Manesh and Santiago have to be careful what they eat.
* Chun isn't allergic to any foods.
* Rory and Lucia are allergic to living creatures.
* Astrid can't drink milk.
* Lucia doesn't need to avoid bees and wasps.
* Santiago can't eat shrimp.

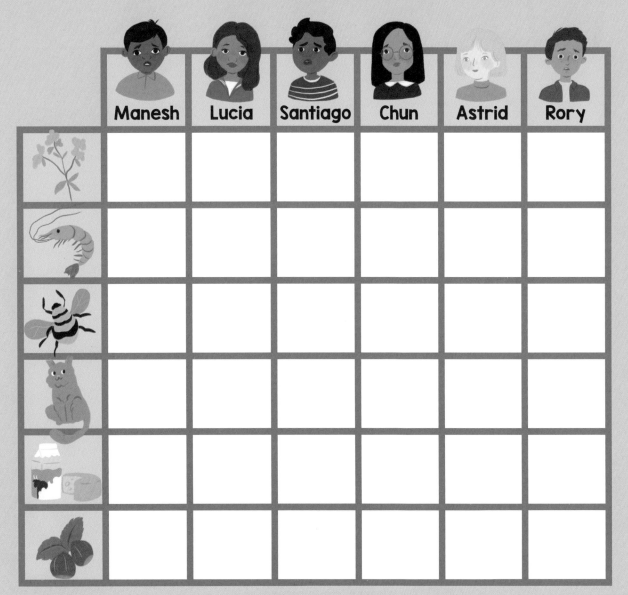

BALANCING ACT

As well as hearing sounds, your ears help you to stay upright and balanced. There is fluid in the inner part of the ear (inside your head) that moves and tells your brain how to keep you balanced. Which of these balancing acts is not dressed in exactly the same costume as the others?

An ear infection can affect your balance. You might feel dizzy, sick, or uncoordinated and be unable to walk and move without wobbling or falling.

MULTIVITAMINS

Most people can get all the vitamins they need from a healthy, varied diet. But some people, including young children, need to take extra vitamins. Find two bottles that add up to exactly four weeks of tablets for one person taking one tablet each day.

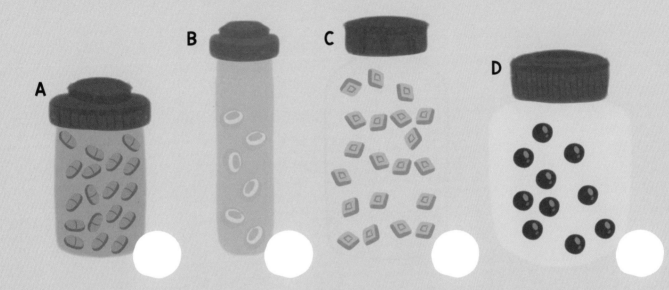

REHYDRATE!

Your body is 60% water! Water makes a huge part of your skin, blood, and internal organs. Put these glasses into pairs. Which two don't match? Now look at the matching pairs; which ones would overflow if you poured one into the other?

Try to drink at least eight glasses of water each day. Your body needs water to carry oxygen to your cells and to get rid of waste, but you lose it through sweating, peeing, and breathing.

Feeling thirsty is a sign you need to rehydrate, but you might also feel tired or dizzy, have a headache, have dry skin or lips, or be unable to concentrate.

LEFT AND RIGHT

The human brain is divided into two halves. Each half controls movements and sensory input (such as touch). However, some areas are special to one side or the other. Find the quickest path through each side and see which one is shorter.

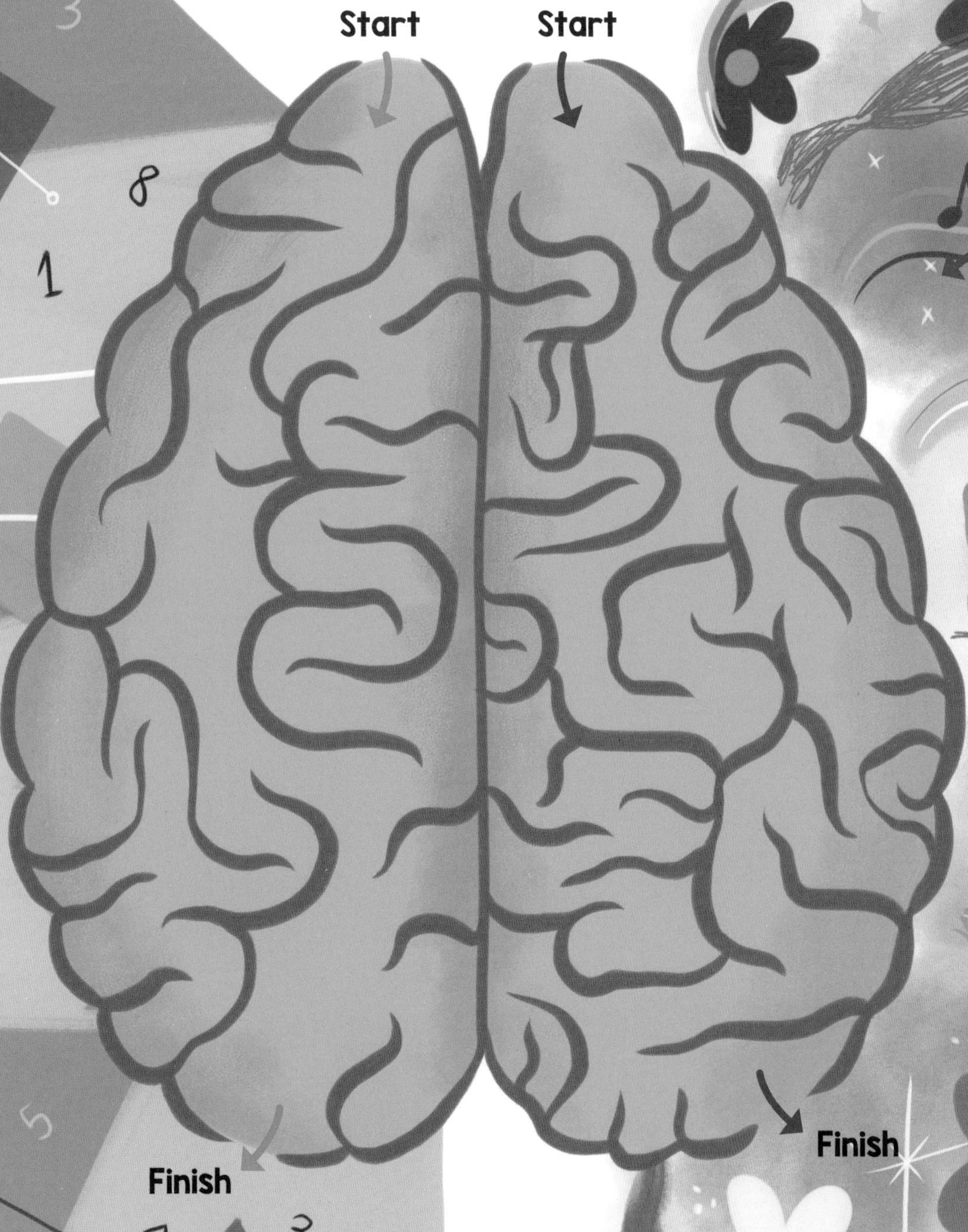

Start   **Start**

Finish

Finish

BUILD IT UP

Proteins are sometimes nicknamed the building blocks of the human body. They help make our bones, muscles, and organs. Fit the proteins back into the lungs by matching the correct shapes. Which one doesn't fit?

Proteins are made up of chains of amino acids with different shapes, sizes and patterns. We get them from the food that we eat.

A   B   C   D   E   F   G   H

TRAIN YOUR BRAIN

How many things can you remember? Put your brain cells to the test with this map task. Remember the directions from the list and then turn the page.

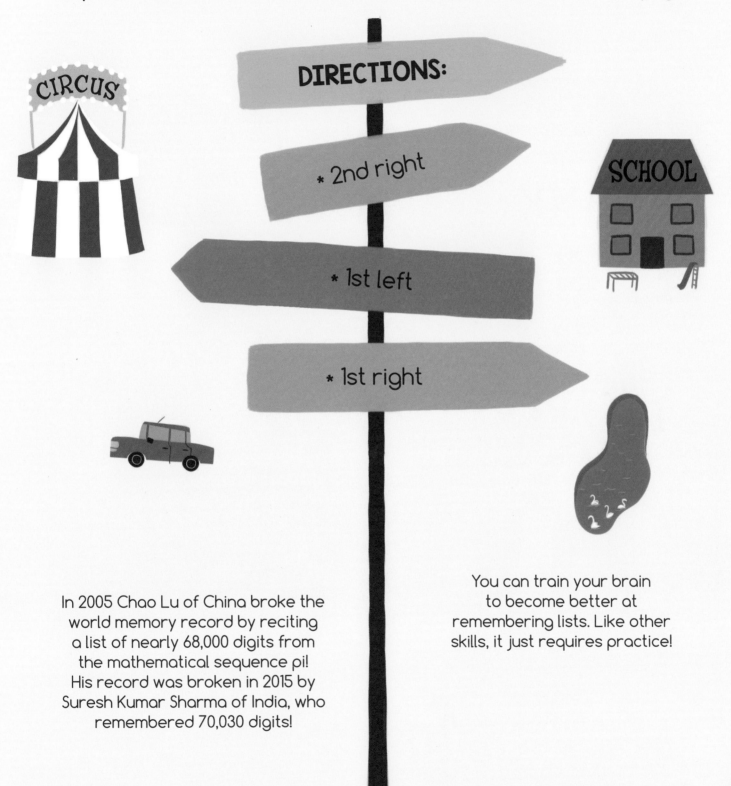

DIRECTIONS:

CIRCUS

SCHOOL

* 2nd right

* 1st left

* 1st right

In 2005 Chao Lu of China broke the world memory record by reciting a list of nearly 68,000 digits from the mathematical sequence pi! His record was broken in 2015 by Suresh Kumar Sharma of India, who remembered 70,030 digits!

You can train your brain to become better at remembering lists. Like other skills, it just requires practice!

MEMORY TEST

Use the memorized directions from the previous page to guide this car around the town. What is the final destination?

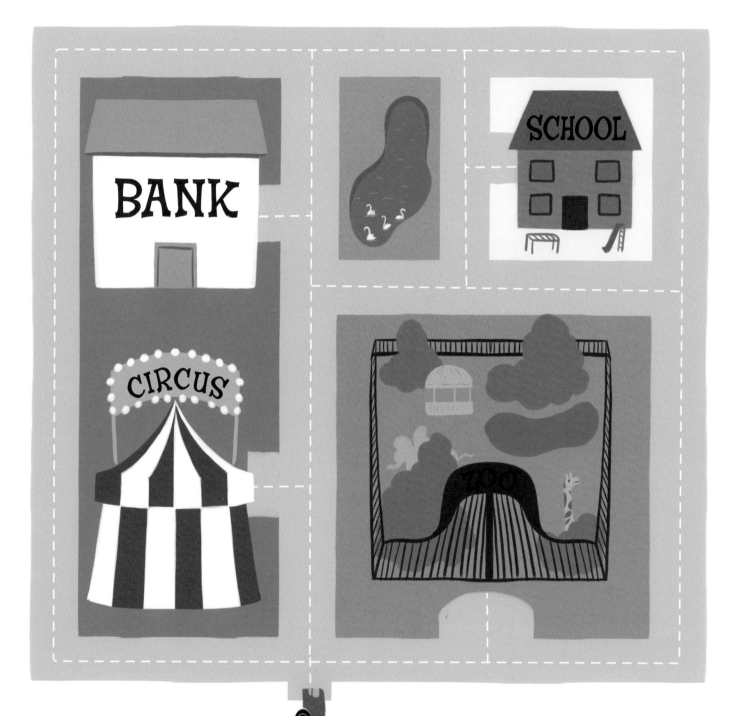

BROKEN BONES

The bones in your body are constantly renewing their cells so you can grow bigger and stay healthy. But what happens when you break a bone?

Felix has broken his leg and is getting it fixed. Can you put the jumbled-up picture pieces in the correct order?

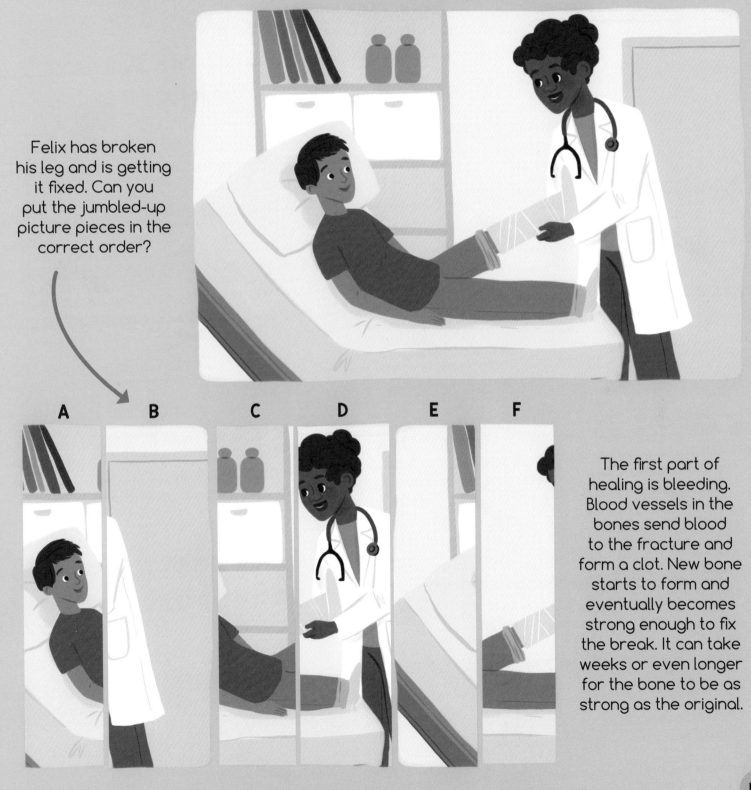

A   B   C   D   E   F

The first part of healing is bleeding. Blood vessels in the bones send blood to the fracture and form a clot. New bone starts to form and eventually becomes strong enough to fix the break. It can take weeks or even longer for the bone to be as strong as the original.

STOP BUGGING ME

A parasite is a creature that lives off another creature. Sounds icky, but humans have them! Mosquitoes and lice both feed on human blood. Yuck! Which are there more of here? And can you spot one of each that is a tiny bit different?

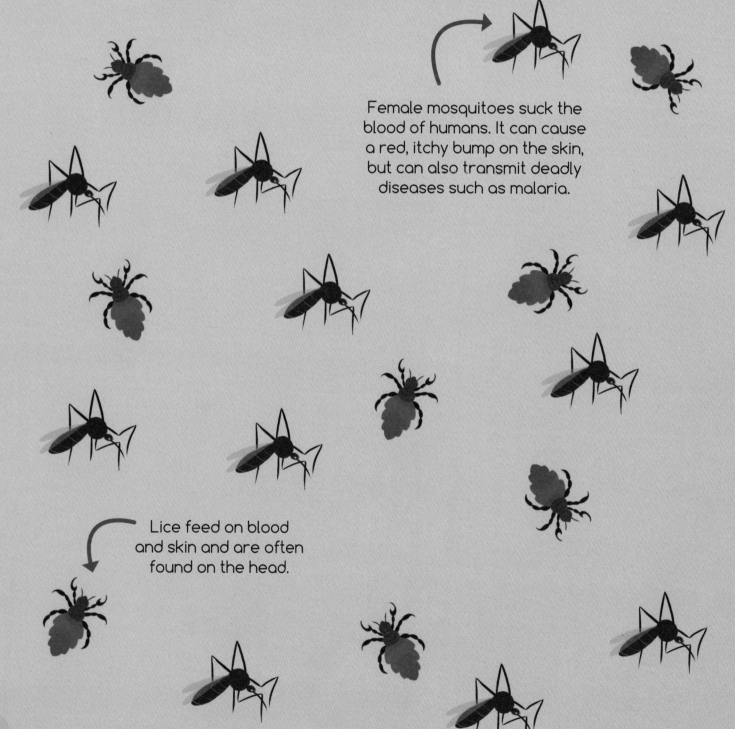

Female mosquitoes suck the blood of humans. It can cause a red, itchy bump on the skin, but can also transmit deadly diseases such as malaria.

Lice feed on blood and skin and are often found on the head.

MUSCLE MATCH

There are more than 600 muscles in the body. Most of them are attached to your bones so that you can move around. Take a look at these two fine figures, and see which of the silhouettes is a match for each one.

Your body also contains cardiac muscle (in your heart) and smooth muscles (in your blood vessels and digestive system, for example) that work in the background without you even thinking about it.

The body contains different types of muscle. The ones you can see when you flex your arm or bend your leg are skeletal muscles. These help you run, jump, sit or lift a glass to your mouth.

WHAT'S THAT NOISE?

The ear you can see is only one part of your hearing system. You also have a middle ear and an inner ear. Finish off this diagram by filling in the missing parts.

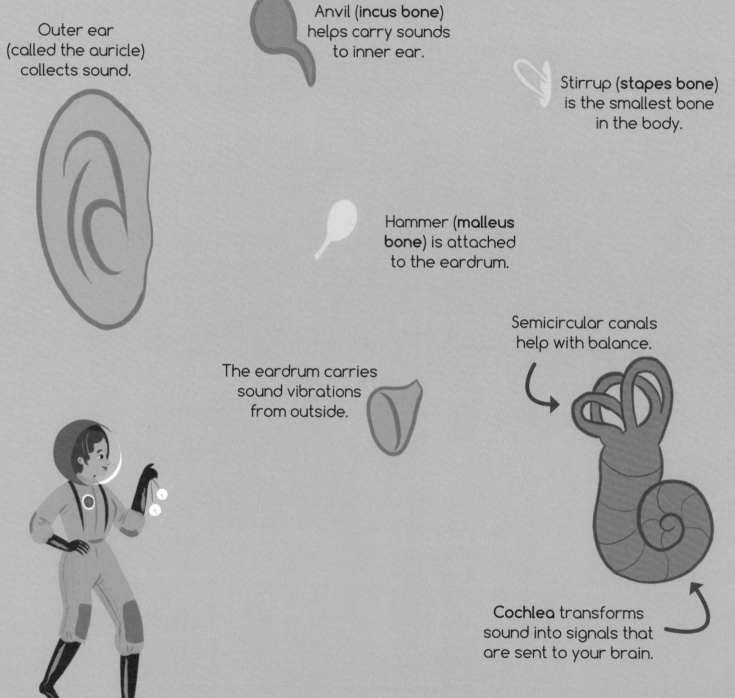

Outer ear (called the auricle) collects sound.

Anvil (**incus bone**) helps carry sounds to inner ear.

Stirrup (**stapes bone**) is the smallest bone in the body.

Hammer (**malleus bone**) is attached to the eardrum.

Semicircular canals help with balance.

The eardrum carries sound vibrations from outside.

Cochlea transforms sound into signals that are sent to your brain.

Earwax is made of oil, sweat, and skin cells. It both protects and cleans your ears. It stops anything from getting inside to the delicate inner part of your ear. And it also removes gunk such as dust and dead skin cells.

There are two types of earlobes, attached and detached. What you have is decided by your genes.

Tinnitus is the peculiar sensation of hearing noises that aren't there. People with tinnitus may have a ringing, buzzing, humming, or whooshing sound in their ear.

WATERWORKS

Our body gets rid of waste in the form of pee and poop, via the urinary system and the digestive system. It gets flushed away to keep us safe from germs. Find out which of these toilets is plumbed in to lead to the sewer system.

The average person produces up to 2 l (3.5 pints) of urine per day. You may visit the toilet more often if you drink a lot of water.

IN AND OUT

Your diaphragm helps you breathe. It also helps your body get rid of vomit, pee, and poop, as well as helping if you lift something heavy. Which is the only group of letters that can be rearranged to spell diaphragm correctly?

PFRGDIAAM

DAGRMIAPH

APHIRAMDM

Hiccups are caused by your diaphragm twitching sharply drawing air into your lungs and making your vocal cords snap shut suddenly.

DIMAPHREG

APHRDIAAM

PIDMAGRAF

The diaphragm is shaped like a parachute and separates your chest and abdomen.

IT'S COLD OUTSIDE!

Shivering is caused by hundreds of muscles contracting at one time. This produces heat and is your body's way of trying to warm up. Can you s-s-s-spot six differences between these p-p-p-pictures?

When you breathe out, your breath contains moisture from your mouth and lungs. In the cold, it forms a little cloud of moisture that is visible.

HOSPITAL HELP

Did you know that there are doctors and medical staff for all kinds of specialist areas? Follow the instructions to complete both heart charts below.

What to do:

* Draw hearts in the squares so that every doctor has at least one heart alongside, either to the side, above, or below.

* A heart cannot be next to or diagonal to another heart. A heart cannot be diagonal to a doctor, either.

* The numbers at the edge tell you how many hearts in each row and column.

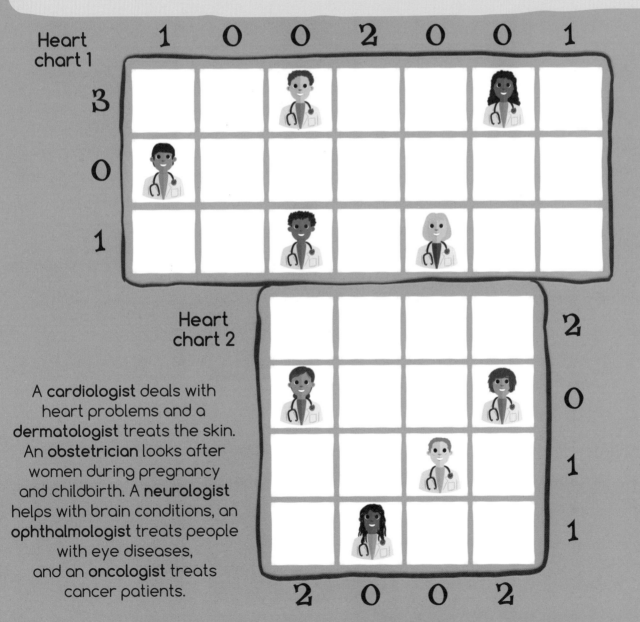

A **cardiologist** deals with heart problems and a **dermatologist** treats the skin. An **obstetrician** looks after women during pregnancy and childbirth. A **neurologist** helps with brain conditions, an **ophthalmologist** treats people with eye diseases, and an **oncologist** treats cancer patients.

TURN IT AROUND!

Researchers studying the brain sometimes test the brain's ability to rotate patterns and objects. For each pair, decide whether the boxes would be identical if you could rotate one of the boxes.

Some people are naturally better at this puzzle than others. However, some conditions affect your brain's ability to perform this task. People suffering from Parkinson's disease may find it hard to work out the answers.

A

B

C
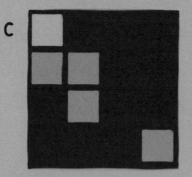

D

THE TASTE TEST

Your mouth can identify five basic tastes: sweet, sour, salty, umami, and bitter. You use taste receptor cells which are found on your tongue in groups, called taste buds. Work out the name of each tasty food and write it in the correct list.

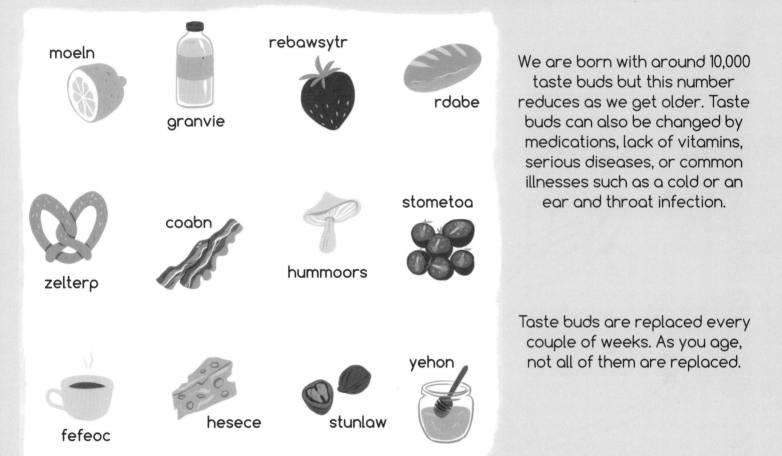

moeln

granvie

rebawsytr

rdabe

zelterp

coabn

hummoors

stometoa

fefeoc

hesece

stunlaw

yehon

We are born with around 10,000 taste buds but this number reduces as we get older. Taste buds can also be changed by medications, lack of vitamins, serious diseases, or common illnesses such as a cold or an ear and throat infection.

Taste buds are replaced every couple of weeks. As you age, not all of them are replaced.

SWEET	SOUR	SALTY	UMAMI	BITTER

LISTEN CAREFULLY

A doctor uses a stethoscope to hear inside a patient's body. They mostly listen to the heart or lungs to check they're working properly. How many stethoscopes can you count in this pile?

The stethoscope was invented in 1819 by the French doctor René Laennec. Modern ones are made up of a disk that is held on the chest, connected by rubber tubes to two earpieces.

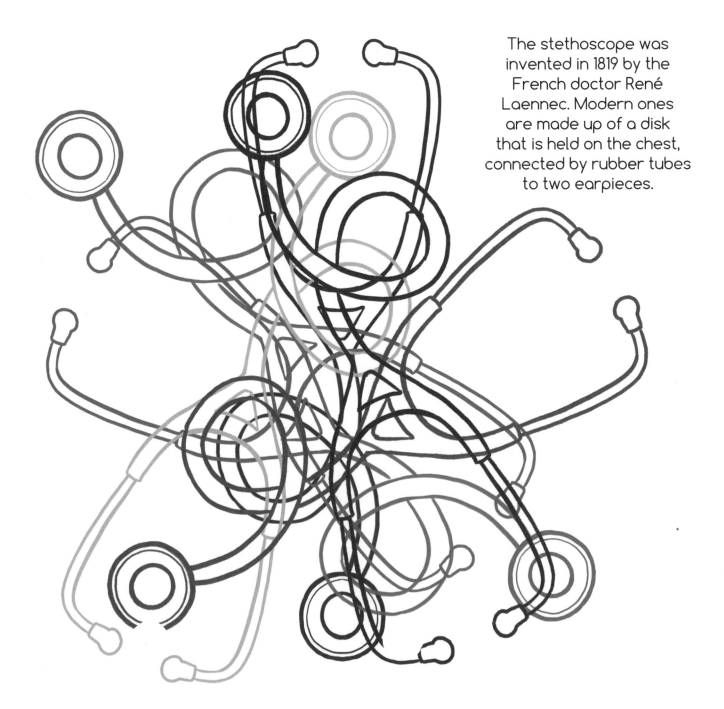

GOING VIRAL

Viruses are tiny parasites that enter your body's cells and make copies of themselves.

Viruses can make you really sick. However, if your body has encountered a virus before, it will remember it —and can quickly fight back!

Viruses are not technically "alive," because they cannot move, grow, or eat.

Test your own memory by studying the viruses in this picture carefully. Then turn the page. Which viruses do you remember?

PART 2 OF GOING VIRAL

Without turning back, which of these viruses do you recognize from the previous page?

Your body can defend itself against viruses. If you get a fever, your body temperature rises and makes it too hot for a virus to reproduce.

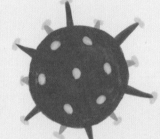

The body's immune system fights viruses, too. It makes antibodies to attack them. Once you are better, the antibodies stay in your body in case they are ever needed again to fight the same virus.

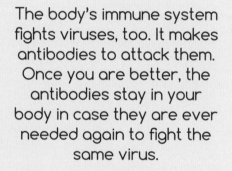

A vaccination teaches your immune system to fight a disease. Vaccinations for viral diseases usually do that by introducing a small part of a virus, or a dead or weakened virus into your body. It doesn't give you the disease, but your body will know how to fight the virus if you come into contact with it afterward.

WHAT'S YOUR TYPE?

Your doctor may test your blood for many reasons. One reason may be to see what blood type you have. Use the clues to work out who has which type below, and what test they had.

There are four main blood types: A, B, AB, and O. All of them can be rhesus positive (+) or rhesus negative (-).

	A+	O+	AB-
JACQUES			
AGNES			
LASSI			

	Cholesterol test	Blood sugars test	Blood type test
JACQUES			
AGNES			
LASSI			

* Jacques and Lassi both have rhesus positive blood.
* Agnes was tested for cholesterol.
* Lassi's blood typing test shows he isn't O group.
* The person with O+ blood type took a blood sugars test.

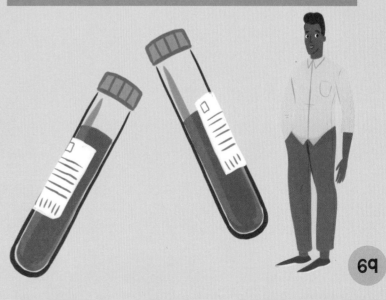

69

SUPER SYSTEMS

The organs of the body can be grouped into systems according to the jobs they do. Use the clues to help you label each of these.

Food passes through the body via the **digestive system**. This system can be divided into several different parts, including the stomach and small and large intestines.

Made up of bones, the **skeletal system** supports the body.

The **circulatory system** consists of the heart, blood, and all your connected arteries and veins. This system moves blood around the body.

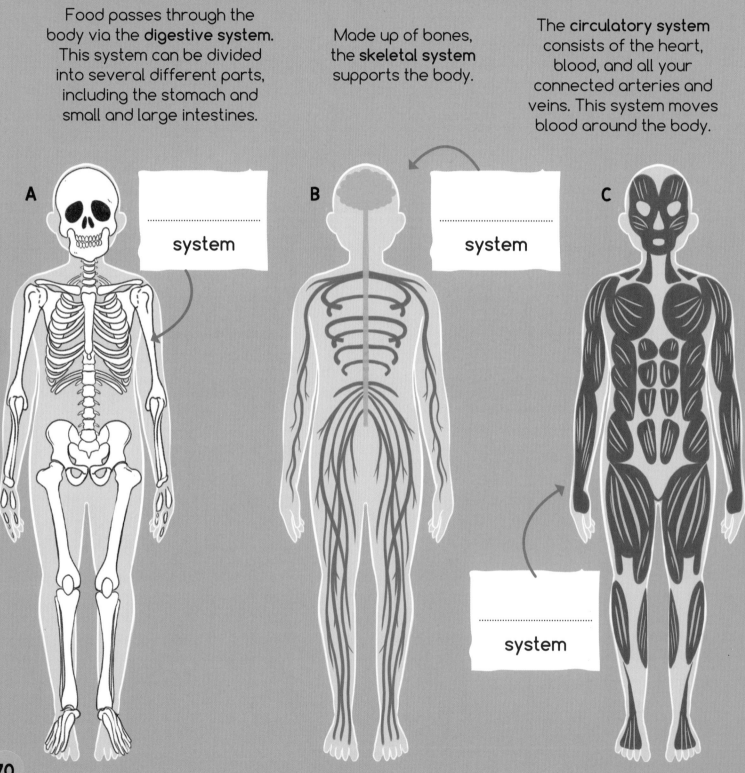

A

....
system

B

....
system

C

....
system

The **nervous system** controls involuntary actions (such as breathing) as well as voluntary actions like running and jumping. The brain is a major part of your **nervous system**.

The **respiratory system** uses the lungs to help you take in oxygen.

There are around 650 muscles in your **muscular system**. Muscles move your limbs, pump blood, and move other substances through your organs.

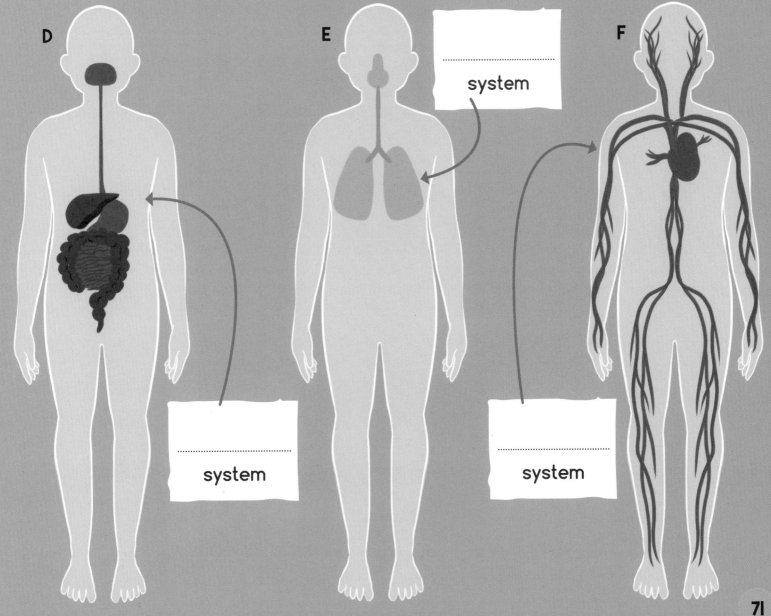

D

E

....
system

system

F

....
system

ON THE INSIDE

Put the missing circles back into this x-ray.
Which one of the circles doesn't fit?

X-rays were used
during World War I to
locate bullets in the
bodies of wounded
soldiers.

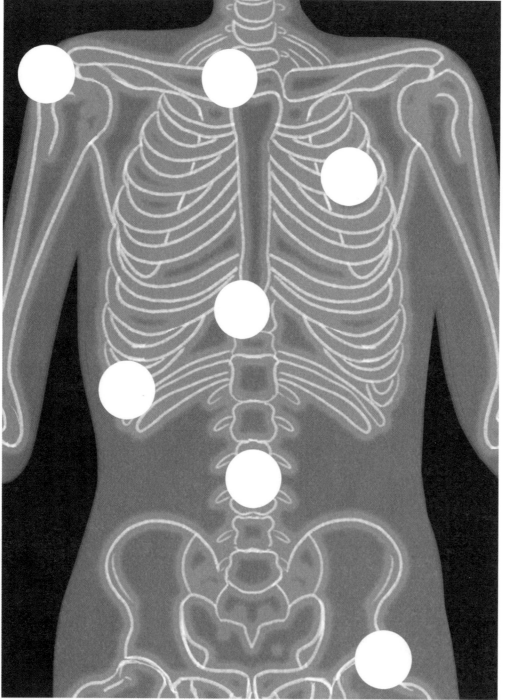

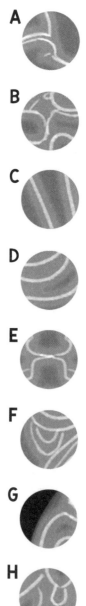

A

B

C

D

E

F

G

H

BEING BORN

A woman is pregnant for around 40 weeks. The baby grows inside her womb until it is ready to be born. Use the clues to work out which of these babies was born first.

Aiko

Jack

Zoe

* Aiko is younger than Jack.
* Cora is older than Jack.
* Laszlo was born after Sudeep but before Aiko.
* Sudeep is the second oldest.
* Zoe was born next after Jack

Sudeep

Laszlo

Cora

Tiny babies have tiny bellies. They need milk every few hours because their stomach is so small. When they are first born, their stomach is around the size of a hazelnut. It grows quickly over the first few days.

BODY BITS

Match the facts to the little pictures, and find a way to fill the grid so that each row, column, and mini-grid contains one of each body part.

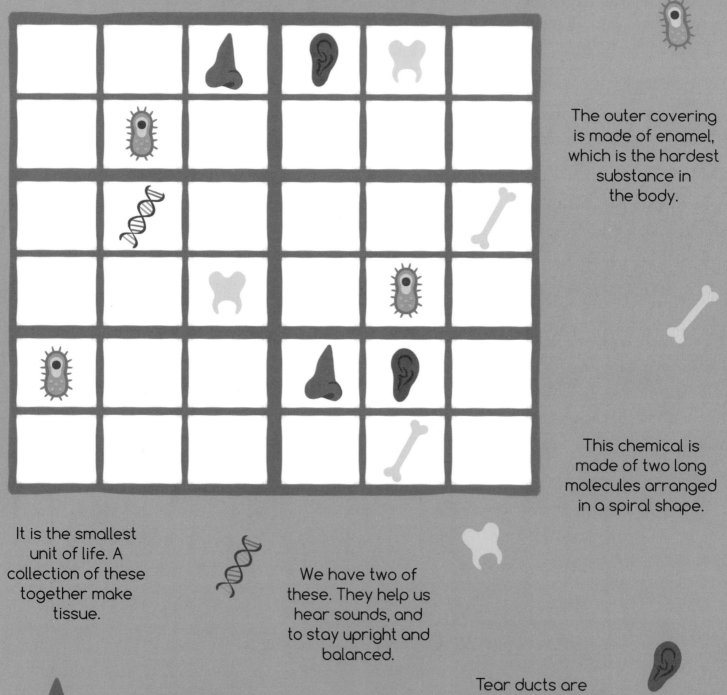

The outer covering is made of enamel, which is the hardest substance in the body.

This chemical is made of two long molecules arranged in a spiral shape.

It is the smallest unit of life. A collection of these together make tissue.

We have two of these. They help us hear sounds, and to stay upright and balanced.

Tear ducts are linked to it.

Your skeleton is made up of 206 of these.

MENU PLANNER

Healthy eating can be simple. It's easy to have a healthy balance of protein, carbs, and vegetables.

Choose a balanced menu that adds up to exactly 500 calories.

30

300

475

Try to eat as many different fruits and vegetables as you can; at least five each day. If you choose to follow a plant-based diet, make sure you get enough protein from soy, lentils, beans, nuts, and seeds.

20

220

250

45

230

35

SPARE PARTS

Modern medicine and surgery are amazing. Transplants allow people to have worn out or diseased parts of the body replaced with healthy ones. Finish off the diagram opposite by filling in the transplanted parts.

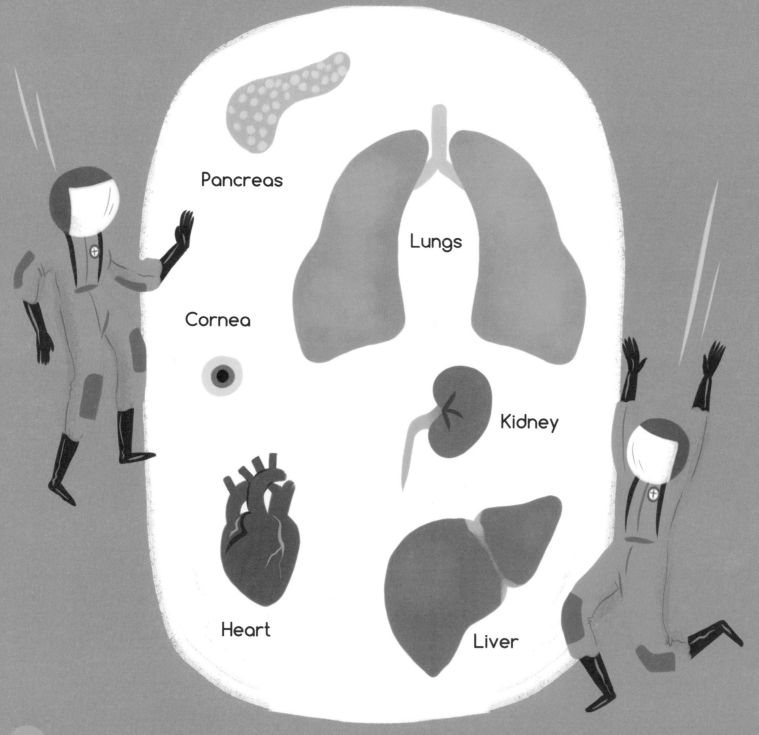

Pancreas

Lungs

Cornea

Kidney

Heart

Liver

The first successful human heart transplant took place in 1967.

One or both kidneys can be replaced with a healthy kidney from another person (known as a donor).

A full liver can regrow from just a part of a liver implanted in a patient.

EXTREME SPORT

Most people can only hold their breath for up to a minute before their body and brain demand more oxygen. Some free divers have trained themselves to hold it for much longer. Which of the divers here looks a little bit different from the others?

The world record for the longest time for a person holding their breath is over 24 minutes.

Holding your breath is difficult because waste gas (carbon dioxide) builds up in your lungs and your body wants to get rid of it.

A person may suffer brain damage if they go without oxygen for too long.

It is easier to hold your breath underwater because of a natural reflex that occurs in the human body. It makes the heart beat more slowly, and the body need less oxygen. However, it is more dangerous to train underwater.

UPSIDE DOWN

Your heart pumps blood around your body. Blood has to reach all the parts, even flowing against gravity to travel up your legs and back to your heart. It works when you're upside down, too!

How many upside-down people can you count in this scene?

Veins carry blood back to your heart. They have valves which open and close to let blood flow through. They only open in one direction to stop blood from going the wrong way— even if you're upside down.

A teenager's heart beats around 60 to 80 times every minute or over 100,000 times per day.

GET FIT!

Exercise is important, whatever your age. It strengthens your muscles and bones, boosts your mood, and lowers the risk of developing many diseases. Work your way around this get fit grid following the instructions.

Instructions:

1. Start in E1. What sport are you playing?
2. Jog two squares up and one square across. What equipment do you need?
3. Run to the monkey bars. What square are they in?
4. Move one down. How many squares should you travel to the right to do some yoga?

One way to tell if you're exercising at the right level is if you can still talk, but not sing.

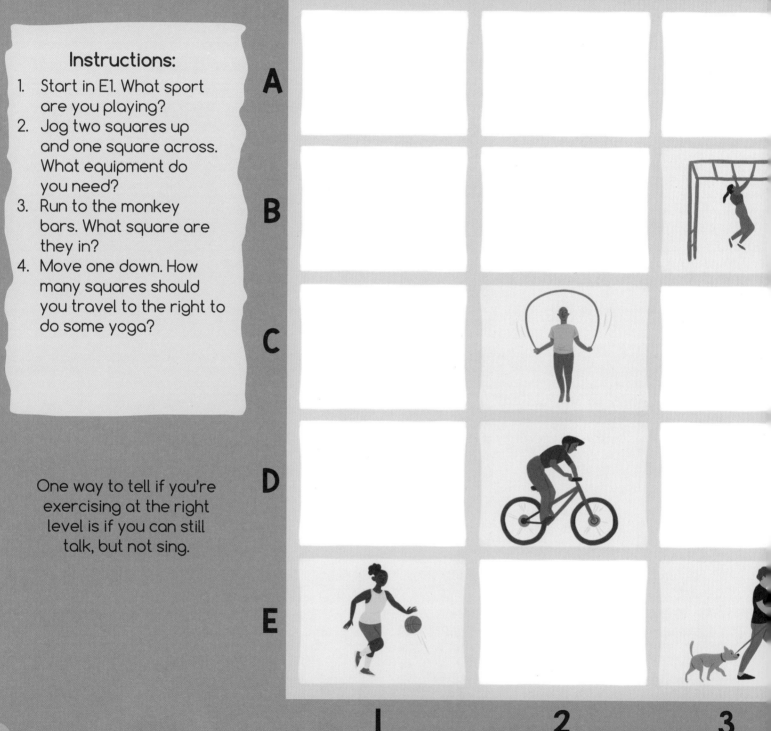

Children and young people should try to do two types of exercise. They should aim for at least 60 minutes of activity each day that makes them sweat and a little bit out of breath. They should also do exercise to develop their balance and flexibility, and build their bone strength and muscle power.

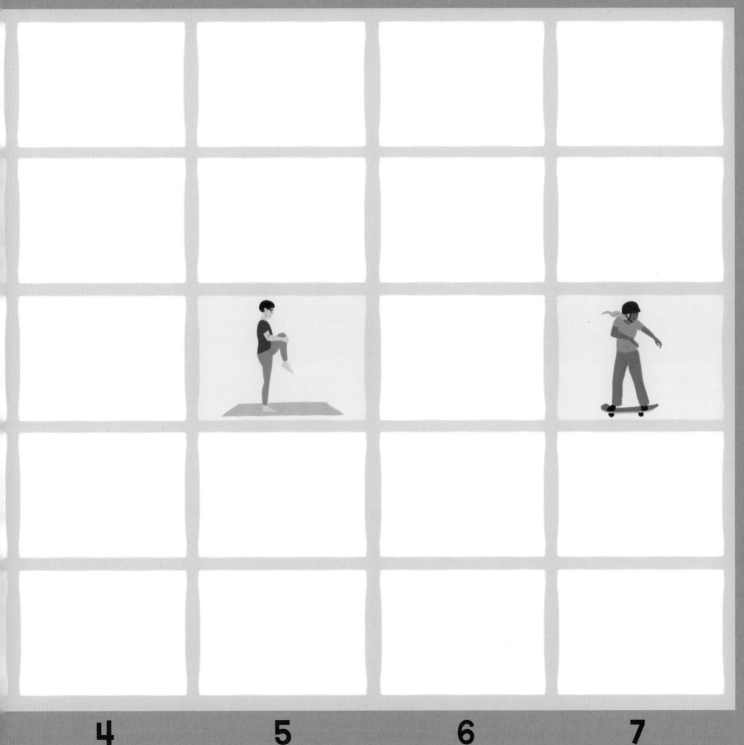

4   5   6   7

GOOSEBUMPS

Wah! Scary things make the hairs on our body stand on end, in the same way we react when we're cold. Take a look at these two scary scenes and see if you can spot eight differences.

Scientists think that we get goosebumps when we're in a frightening situation because of a nervous response. It prepares us to defend ourselves against an attacker. The puffed-up hairs (or fur, in other animals) makes us look bigger and more dangerous.

WEIGHT A MINUTE

Welcome to the gym! It's time to do some heavy lifting ... with your brain. Find a path through the kettlebells following the 8 times table in the correct order. You can move to the side, and up and down, but not diagonally.

Start

4	16	8	20	20	12	8	14
4	24	22	28	32	16	16	30
20	32	38	40	42	44	36	12
24	40	48	56	64	73	78	84
48	28	10	70	72	69	76	65
6	73	96	88	80	98	88	84
112	90	104	108	126	48	130	124
108	100	112	124	104	130	115	110

Finish

The human body is designed to stand upright, but today's lifestyle sees us sitting down for long periods—at a desk, on the sofa, while we eat, text, and play video games. Swinging a kettlebell is a great exercise to keep us moving. If you don't have one, just remember to get up, stand tall, stretch, and move about.

IN YOUR DREAMS

Researchers believe that everyone dreams, every night, but we don't all remember our dreams. Follow the paths to see who is dreaming about what tonight.

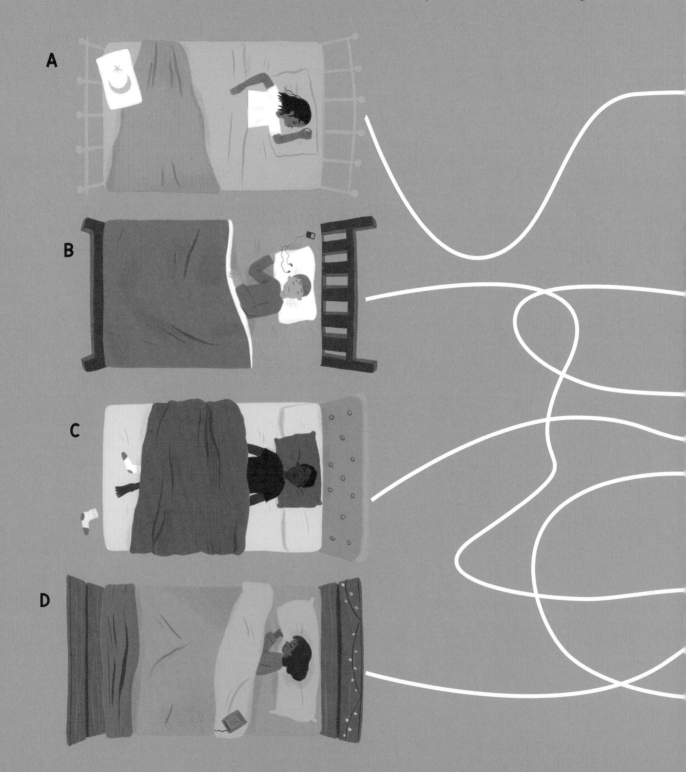

Dreams usually involve real events and people, but all mixed up together. They will quite often be things from the past couple of days.

Are your dreams a little bit crazy? Scientists think it's because the front part of our brain, which controls how we make sense of the world, shuts down during dreams. The other parts of our brain take over and put things together that don't normally go.

BLACK AND WHITE

A newborn baby's eyesight is nowhere near as good as an adult's. Bold, contrasting images are the easiest things for them to see as their eyes develop. Look at each group of pictures and spot the odd one out each time.

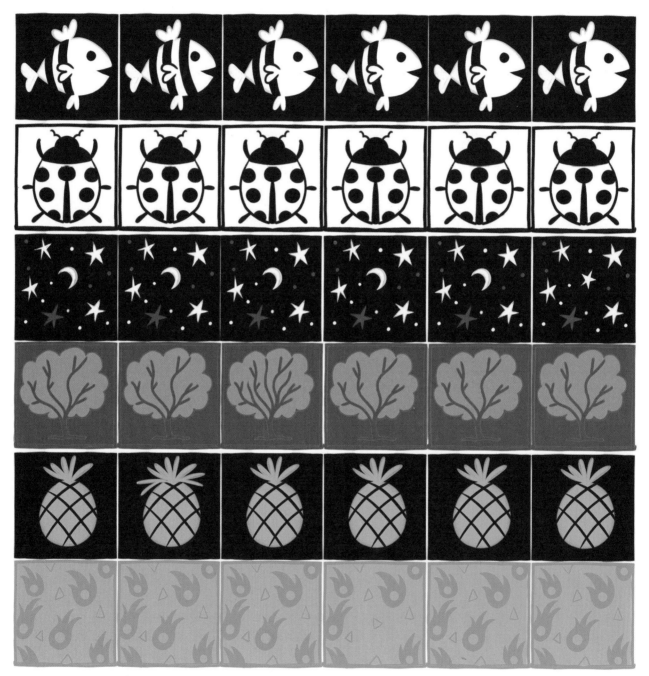

A baby's eyes see black, white, and red before developing to be able to tell red and green apart. Then they see blue and yellow. The brighter the shade, the better they see it.

ANSWERS

Page 4

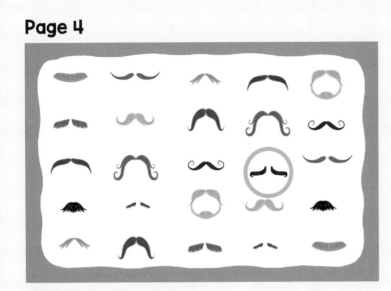

Page 5

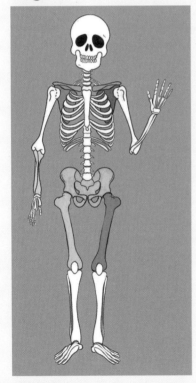

Page 6

There are 7 thermometers.

Page 7

= 16   = 14   = 20

Page 8-9

Page 10

Page 11

From oldest to youngest:
Jim, Betty, Ernest, Claude, Janet, Anjali.

Page 12

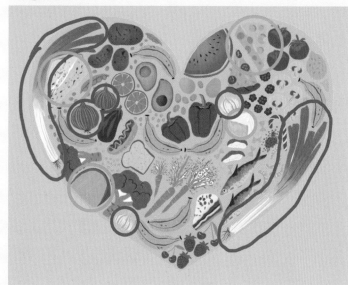

There are 7 bananas.
The red fruit and vegetables are strawberries, cherries, red bell peppers, and tomatoes.

Page 13

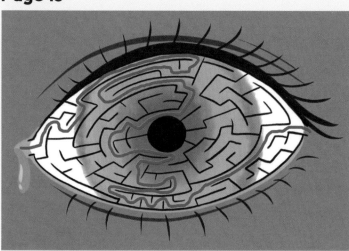

Page 14

This germ is the most common.

Page 15

Page 16

Box D contains all of the parts.

Page 17

The bit that separates your nostrils is called the SEPTUM.
The groove above your top lip is called the PHILTRUM.

Page 18

Tiles B, D, F, G, and J are not from the family portrait.

Page 20

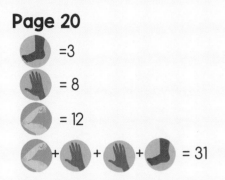 = 3

= 8

= 12

+ + + = 31

Page 21

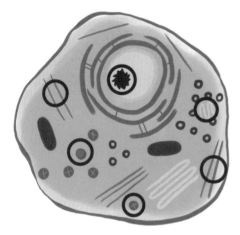

Page 22
F

Page 23
Megan has smelled blue cheese.

Page 24

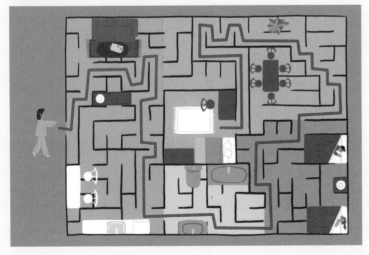

Page 26

 = 5

= 2

= 3

= 6

Page 27

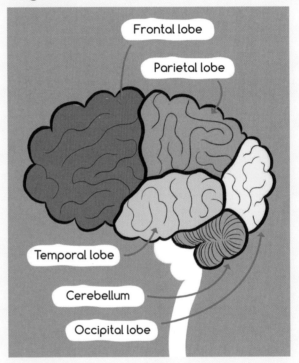

Page 28
Prints A and F were not made by this person.

Page 29

There are 50 cells in total.

25 cells should have stars on them.

5 cells should have a cross on them.

5 cells should have a circle on them.

There should be 15 cells with no markings on them.

Page 30

She sees image A.

Page 31

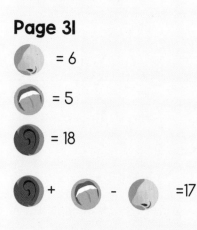

 = 6

= 5

= 18

+ − =17

Page 32

Page 34

	Hockey	Basketball	Swimming
Ethan			✔
Angela	✔		
Teresa		✔	

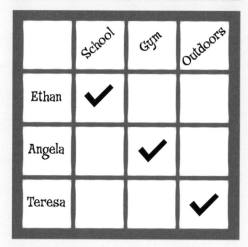

	School	Gym	Outdoors
Ethan	✔		
Angela		✔	
Teresa			✔

Page 35

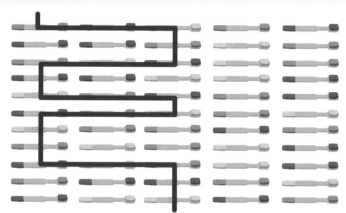

Page 36

A and F are identical.

Page 38

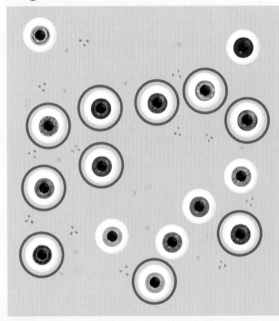

These eyes appear on both pages.

Page 39
LETSKEON

Page 40

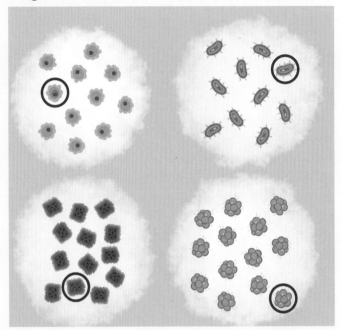

Page 41
1 cervical and 2 thoracic bones are missing.

Page 43
Tiles B, E, G, H, and J are not from the picture.

Page 44
C is the same DNA strand but upside down.

Page 45

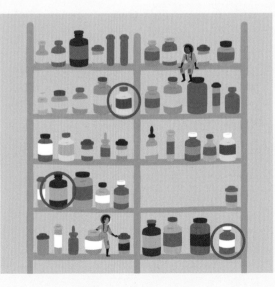

Page 46

There are 4 canine teeth, 5 incisors, and 3 molars.

Page 47

Manesh—nuts.
Lucia—cats.
Santiago—shellfish.
Chun—pollen.
Astrid—dairy.
Rory—bees.

Page 48

Page 49

A and D add up to 28, which is the number of tablets needed for 4 weeks.

Page 50

F and M don't match.
These pairs would overflow if one was poured into the other: B and P, D and J, K and N.

Page 51

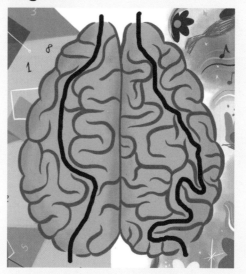

The left side has the shortest path.

Page 52

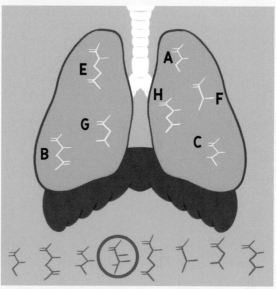

D doesn't fit.

Page 54

If your memory served you well, you should have reached the school.

Page 55
They go in this order: E, A, C, F, D, B.

Page 56
There are more mosquitoes than lice.
These ones are a tiny bit different:

Page 57

Page 58-59

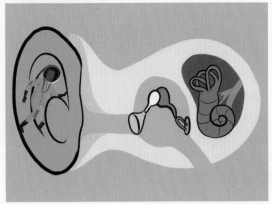

Page 60
B

Page 61
DAGRMIAPH

Page 62

Page 63

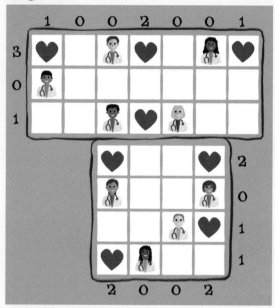

Page 64

Pair B would not be identical if one box rotated

Page 65

SWEET—strawberry, honey.
SOUR—lemon, vinegar.
SALTY—pretzel, bacon, bread.
UMAMI—cheese, mushroom, tomatoes.
BITTER—coffee, walnuts.

Page 66

There are 6 stethoscopes.

Page 68

These viruses are the same:

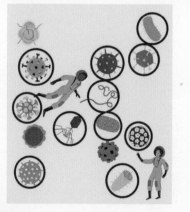

Page 69

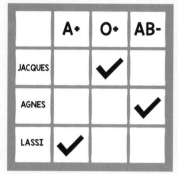

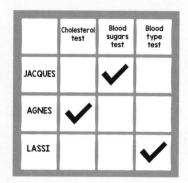

	A+	O+	AB-
JACQUES		✔	
AGNES			✔
LASSI	✔		

	Cholesterol test	Blood sugars test	Blood type test
JACQUES		✔	
AGNES	✔		
LASSI			✔

Page 70-71

A—skeletal system.
B—nervous system.
C—muscular system.
D—digestive system.
E—respiratory system.
F—circulatory system.

Page 72

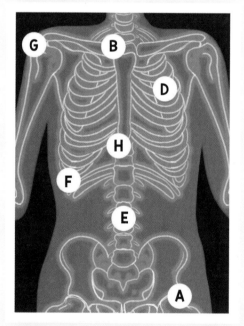

Circle C doesn't fit.

Page 73

Cora was born first, then Sudeep, Jack, Zoe, Laszlo, and finally Aiko.

Page 74

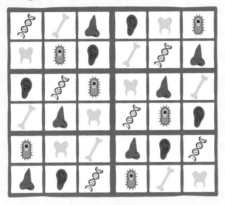

 DNA—This chemical is made of two long molecules arranged in a spiral shape.

Tooth—The outer covering is made of enamel, which is the hardest substance in the body.

Bone—Your skeleton is made up of 206 of these.

Ear—We have two of these. They help us hear sounds, and to stay upright and balanced.

Nose—Tear ducts are linked to it.

Cell—It is the smallest unit of life. A collection of these together make tissue.

Page 75

These foods add up to 500 calories:
salmon (cooked fillet) 230
broccoli 20
sweet potato wedges 250

or you might prefer:
salmon (cooked fillet) 230
broccoli 20
green beans 30
noodles 220

Page 76

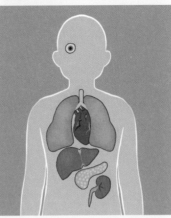

Page 78

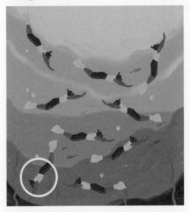

Page 79

There are 4 upside-down people.

Page 80

1. Basketball
2. A rope
3. B3
4. 2 squares

Page 82

Page 83

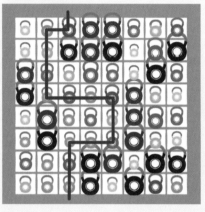

Page 84

A is dreaming about winning a trophy.
B is dreaming about flying.
C is dreaming about a bear and a goat sailing.
D is dreaming about a party.

Page 86

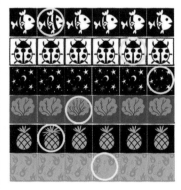